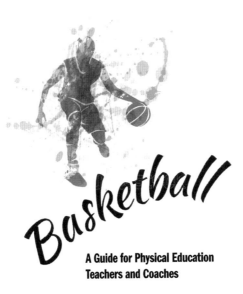

Basketball

A Guide for Physical Education Teachers and Coaches

Basketball

A Guide for Physical Education Teachers and Coaches

Koh Koon Teck
Nanyang Technological University, Singapore

John Wang Chee Keng
Nanyang Technological University, Singapore

World Scientific

NEW JERSEY · LONDON · SINGAPORE · BEIJING · SHANGHAI · HONG KONG · TAIPEI · CHENNAI · TOKYO

Published by

World Scientific Publishing Co. Pte. Ltd.

5 Toh Tuck Link, Singapore 596224

USA office: 27 Warren Street, Suite 401-402, Hackensack, NJ 07601

UK office: 57 Shelton Street, Covent Garden, London WC2H 9HE

National Library Board, Singapore Cataloguing in Publication Data
Name: Koh, Koon Teck. | Wang, John Chee Keng, author.
Title: Basketball : a guide for physical education teachers and coaches /
  Koh Koon Teck, John Wang Chee Keng.
Description: Singapore : World Scientific Publishing Co. Pte Ltd., [2020] |
  Includes index.
Identifier(s): OCN 1141213162 | ISBN 978-981-121-985-6 (paperback) |
  978-981-121-933-7 (hardcover)
Subject(s): LCSH: Basketball--Coaching. | Basketball--Training.
Classification: DDC 796.32307--dc23

British Library Cataloguing-in-Publication Data
A catalogue record for this book is available from the British Library.

Copyright © 2020 by World Scientific Publishing Co. Pte. Ltd.

All rights reserved. This book, or parts thereof, may not be reproduced in any form or by any means, electronic or mechanical, including photocopying, recording or any information storage and retrieval system now known or to be invented, without written permission from the publisher.

For photocopying of material in this volume, please pay a copying fee through the Copyright Clearance Center, Inc., 222 Rosewood Drive, Danvers, MA 01923, USA. In this case permission to photocopy is not required from the publisher.

For any available supplementary material, please visit
https://www.worldscientific.com/worldscibooks/10.1142/11800#t=suppl

Desk Editors: Dr. Sree Meenakshi Sajani/Daniele Lee

Typeset by Stallion Press
Email: enquiries@stallionpress.com

Printed in Singapore

About the Authors

Koon Teck Koh is Associate Professor in the Academic Group of Physical Education & Sports Science at National Institute of Education, Nanyang Technological University (NTU) in Singapore. His research areas are in coach education and sport pedagogy. He has published more than 40 international peer-reviewed papers and book chapters. He has also conducted numerous workshops and coaching courses to build the capacity of physical educators, basketball coaches, co-curriculum activities teachers and athletes.

Koon Teck has been a Physical Education (PE) teacher since 1993. He had taught PE at pre-university and secondary school levels for 10 years. He was Head of Department (PE/CCA) for 6 years before he joined Co-Curricular Activities Branch, Education Programmes Division as advisor and consultant for sports in 2004. He was the advisor for the North Zone Primary Schools Sports Council and South Zone Schools Sports Council. Also, he was the games advisor for basketball overseeing the management and organisation of the games at all levels for different age groups of students.

Koon Teck is actively involved in Basketball as both a competitive athlete and coach at various levels. His keen research areas are in coaching and teaching in PE and Sport, in particular, understanding and developing coaches and PE teachers to promote good practices. He has worked with the Singapore senior basketball team as a team manager and sport scientist to achieve a historical medal at the South East Asia Games in 2013 after 34 years where the last medal was won and maintained the same result at the same competition in 2015.

Since 2002, Koon Teck has involved in Coach Education Programmes (currently termed as SG-Coach). He lectures the theory and technical courses in the National Coaching Accreditation Programme (NCAP) managed by SSC and BAS. Notably, he initiated an integrated NCAP Level 1 Coaching Course for BAS in 2007.

It was the first among the NSAs in Singapore, which combined Theory and Technical courses to promote context-specific learning experience for basketball coaches. He has shared the model with local and international practitioners and researchers.

Dr. Koh holds key appointments at the international and local levels such as Executive Board Member (FIBA Asia Representative), World Association for Basketball Coaches; Executive Board Member, Asia Association of Coaching Science; President, Singapore Physical Education Association; and Honorary Secretary, Basketball Association of Singapore. He is also an Associate Editor of the *Asia Pacific Journal of Education*, as well as Editorial Board Member of the *International Sport Coaching Journal*.

John Chee Keng Wang started his career as a PE teacher and Basketball coach in a secondary school. He is now a Professor in the Physical Education and Sports Science Academic Group at the National Institute of Education (NIE), Nanyang Technological University in Singapore. He received his Ph.D. (Sport and Exercise Psychology) in 2001 from Loughborough University. Dr. Wang is a Chartered Psychologist and an Associate Fellow of British Psychological Society. He is registered with the Health and Care Professions Council of UK as a Sport and Exercise Psychologist. He leads the Motivation in Educational Research Lab (MERL) in NIE.

Contents

About the Authors   v

Chapter One   A Brief History of Basketball   1

Chapter Two   Equipment and Facilities   5

The Basketball Court   6

Chapter Three   Playing Positions   7

Point Guard   7
Shooting Guard   7
Small Forward   8
Power Forward   8
Centre   8

Chapter Four   The Basic Rules   11

Game Length   11
Starting the Game   12
Possession Arrow   13

Out of Court 13
Field Goal 14
Free Throw or Foul Shots 14
Fouls 15
Substitutions 16
Time-outs 16
Inbound the Ball 17
Travelling 17
Double Dribble 18
Back Court 18

Chapter Five   Teaching/Coaching Approaches   23

Traditional and Games Approach 23
Game-Based Approach 24
Modifying Games 31
Some Examples of Modified Games 31

Chapter Six   Suggested Teaching/Coaching Sequences   35

Ball Handling 36
Basic Individual Offensive Skills 42
Basic Individual Defensive Skills 86
Basic Offensive Team Tactics 94
Motion Offence 113
Basic Defensive Team Tactics 117

Chapter Seven   FIBA 3 × 3: Modified Game   123

FIBA 3 × 3: Rules of the Game 123

Chapter Eight Samples of Basketball Skills Rubric 127

Fundamental Basketball Skills 127
Technique Assessment Use Rubrics 129
Rebounding (Without Opponent) 130
Scoring for Rebounding 131
One-Handed Set Shot 132
Scoring for One-Handed Set Shot 133
Layup 134
Scoring for Layup 135
Gameplay Assessment Use Rubrics 136

Chapter Nine Sample Lesson Plans 139

Sample Lesson Plan 1 139
Sample Lesson Plan 2 158

References 175

Congratulatory Notes 177

Index 183

CHAPTER ONE
A Brief History of Basketball

Basketball was invented at the International YMCA Training School Springfield (today, Springfield College), Massachusetts, USA in 1891. The man who invented the game was Dr. James A. Naismith, a Canadian-born and Physical Education instructor at the college. At the request from Dr. Luther Gulick, the head of Physical Education at the college, James was given 14 days to create an indoor game that would provide an "athletic distraction" for a rowdy class through the brutal New England winter.

Naismith's invention didn't come easily. He tried many ideas, modified outdoor games such as soccer and lacrosse, but all these games were not suitable for indoor. Getting close to the deadline, James recalled a childhood game that required players to use finesse and accuracy to become successful. After brainstorming his new idea, James developed basketball game with 13 rules.

In the very first game, Dr. Naismith used a soccer ball and attached two peach baskets to the balcony at each end of the gymnasium. The bottoms were left in the basket at first and the balls would have to be retrieved by climbing a stepladder when a goal is made. It started with just 18 men.

The new game spread rapidly and was soon being played across the United States and in many other countries, now it is one of the most popular games in the world with more than 300 million players. Basketball is a popular spectator sport in America today, and through the Olympic Games, it is gaining international interest with more than 200 nations playing the game.

Interesting facts for students:

1. Canadian James Naismith, a PE teacher at a YMCA in Springfield, Massachusetts, is credited with inventing basketball in 1891.
2. The first basketball game was played on a court that was half the size of courts today. Only one point was scored in the whole match. In this game, there were nine players in each team. A number that was based on the standard number of players on a baseball team. Later, the teams were reduced to five players on the court.

3. The first basketball hoops were peach baskets with the bottom intact. Officials had to get the ball out after each basket using stepladder. The first string nets were used in the early 1900s.
4. Early basketball games used soccer balls (1891–1950s). Players would rub coal dust on their hands to grip the ball better.
5. Basketball became popular in high schools of USA before television started to cover national level matches.
6. In 1932, the International Basketball Federation was formed by representatives from Italy, Greece, Argentina, Portugal, Czechoslovakia, Latvia, Romania, and Switzerland. Its acronym is actually FIBA and was taken from the French Fédération Internationale de Basketball Amateur.
7. The game became an official Olympic event at the Summer Games in Berlin, Germany in 1936.
8. Michael Jordan is considered a legend in the world of basketball. Exceptionally talented, Michael Jordan has led the US team in Olympics that won gold medals in 1984 and 1992. Michael Jordan's career score is 32,292, this is after Kareem Abdul-Jabbar (38,387), Karl Malone (36,928), Kobe Bryant (33,643), and LeBron James (32,543). His record total career playoffs score of 5,987 in NBA was only broken recently by LeBron James (6,911).

9. Kareem Abdul-Jabbar holds the record for highest score of career points, i.e., 38,387 in the history of NBA. He played for the Milwaukee Bucks and Los Angeles Lakers.
10. The Naismith Memorial Basketball Hall of Fame is located in Springfield, Massachusetts, USA.
11. The Harlem Globetrotters are a world famous exhibition basketball team. They combine athleticism, theatre, and comedy in their style of play. They have been entertaining fans since they were formed in 1926. This popular team has played more than 26,000 games in 124 countries as of 2019. They are not part of the NBA.
12. Wang Zhizhi—not Yao Ming—was the first Chinese player to compete in the NBA. He was a 7'0" centre and played his first NBA game for the Dallas Mavericks in the 2000–2001 season.

CHAPTER TWO
Equipment and Facilities

Player should wear proper court shoes and comfortable attire to enable them to have a freedom of movement such as run, jump, and shoot.

The Basketball Court

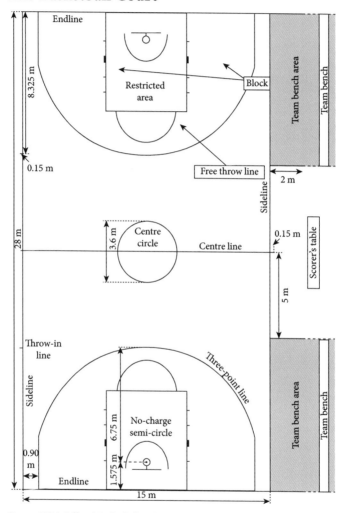

Source: FIBA Official Basketball Rules (2014).

CHAPTER THREE
Playing Positions

Point Guard

The point guard is the floor leader on offence. He controls the tempo of the attack and has a good understanding of his teammates, in terms of their strengths and roles. The point guard is usually the quickest player in the team with the best ball handling skills, great peripheral vision and greater shooting range. When defending, the point guard must be able to slow down the opponent's team point guard.

Shooting Guard

A shooting guard must be a good shooter from short and long range, and fastbreaks. In addition, the shooting guard should be able to help the point guard in ball control at times and pass the ball to teammate at the low post. When defending, the shooting guard will guard the best perimeter player of the attacking team.

Small Forward

The small forward is usually the fittest player in the team who operate on wings and baseline areas as well as in the blocks or near the restricted area for rebounding (recover ball after a missed shot). He is able to shoot from outside, drive the ball into the rim, and fast breaks. When defending, the small forward should be able to guard both big and small players.

Power Forward

The power forward makes big contributions without the ball in his hands, for example, to set up screens, boxes out, rebounding. He should be a good free throw shooter as he will draw a lot of contacts during play.

Centre

The centre is usually the tallest player in the team. The centre will play very close to the basket to best utilise his height for attack and rebound. The centre player is most influential in attaching as well as defending.

Although some players were born to play specific positions, most players develop their skills through training and practice. It is important to build all-rounded players rather than to restrict the skills development to player's position.

CHAPTER FOUR
The Basic Rules

Basketball rules are designed to make the game run smoothly and safely so that everyone can enjoy and compete in a safe manner. The rules are set for fair play. Players should be familiar with the basic rules to ensure fair and safe play.

Game Length

A game consists of four quarters of 10 minutes. There is an interval of 2 minutes between first and second quarter, and between third and fourth quarter. Usually, there is a longer interval at half time (10–15 minutes) before the third quarter begins. Timing rules may vary depending on the level of competition. There is a pre-game on court warm-up period of around 15 minutes before the start of the game. If the score is tied at the end of the fourth quarter, the game shall continue with as many overtimes of 5 minutes duration each as necessary to break the tie.

Starting the Game

For all games, the first team named in the schedule (home team) shall have the team bench and its own basket on the left side of the scorer's table, facing the playing court. However, if the two teams agree, they may interchange the team benches and/or baskets. Before the first and third quarter, teams are entitled to warm-up in the half of the playing court in which their opponents' basket is located. Teams shall exchange baskets for the second half. In all overtimes, the teams shall continue to play towards the same baskets as in the fourth quarter.

The match starts with five players from each team on the court.

The game will start off with a jump ball at the centre court, usually between the team's centres (or anyone from the team). The other eight players must stand outside the circle until one or both players tap the ball. Neither jumper may catch the ball or tap it more than twice until it has touched one of the non-jumpers or the floor. If the ball is not tapped by at least one of the jumpers, the jump ball shall be repeated. The "jumper" cannot catch the ball.

Possession Arrow

When two players from the opposing teams have possession of the ball simultaneously and cannot get free, a "jump ball" may be called by the referee. In this case, teams alternate possession. The "possession arrow" can be found at the scorer's table. The possession arrow changes every time when a jump ball situation is called by the referee. The team that did not win the first jump ball takes the ball out of bounds in the next jump ball situation. The team entitled to the next alternating possession at the end of any quarter or overtime shall begin the next quarter or overtime with a throw-in from the centre line extended, opposite the scorer's table, unless there are further free throws and a possession penalty to be administered. If a player(s) move(s) to out-of-bounds or to his backcourt during a held ball, a jump ball situation occurs.

Out of Court

The ball is considered out of court when it touches on the sideline, baseline, or outside of the court.

The throw (in bound) is taken from where the ball is out of play.

The ball is out-of-bounds when it touches:

1. A player or any other person who is out-of-bounds.
2. The floor or any object above, on or outside the boundary line.
3. The backboard supports, the back of the backboards, or any object above the playing court.

Field Goal

A field goal is any basket scored by throwing the ball through the ring/basket during the course of play. If the ball is scored inside the 3-point perimeter, the goal is worth 2 points. Otherwise, it will be 3 points if the shot is successful.

After a successful field goal, the defending team must throw the ball back into play (in bound) behind any part of the baseline of their opponent's basket (within 5 seconds upon holding the ball).

Free Throw or Foul Shots

A player committed a foul while trying to stop his opponent from scoring a field goal illegally. Under such situation, two/three free throws will be awarded to the opponent to be taken behind the free throw line. Only the player who was fouled can take the shots (however, if the player who was fouled cannot attempt the free throw(s) due to injury, the substitution for him shall attempt the free throw(s) on his behalf). Each foul shot is worth one point. If the last shot taken is missed, the game continues as if the player had taken shot in normal play. If the last free throw is scored, the opposing team will start the play from behind the baseline.

Fouls

Deliberate contact to disrupt an opposition player is called a personal foul. Generally, (1) the first player to establish position on the court has priority to that position, (2) a body part cannot be extended into the path of an opponent, and (3) the player who moves into the opponent's path and created a contact is illegal.

Each personal foul will contribute to a team foul. In a regular game, if a team accumulated four team fouls in a quarter, two free throws will be awarded to the opposition team for the subsequent foul(s) committed.

In a 40-minute game, a player can accumulate up to five personal fouls before being disqualified (fouled out) from the game. A substitute is allowed to replace the player who fouled out of the game. A player shall be disqualified for the remainder of the game when he is charged with 2 technical fouls, or 2 unsportsmanlike fouls, or with 1 unsportsmanlike foul and 1 technical foul.

Substitutions

Substitution can be made in the following instances:

1. any time a foul is called,
2. any time the team has sideline possession,
3. a jump ball,
4. at time-outs,
5. when the opposition substitutes on their sideline possession,
6. if a player is injured,
7. half-time or quarter time.

Time-outs

A coach can call two time-outs during first half and three time-outs during the second half of a 40-minute game. Unused time-outs may not be carried over to the next half or overtime. A time-out can be requested by the coach from the scorer's table any time the referee blows the whistle or when the opposition scores a basket. One minute is allowed for a time-out.

Each team may be granted:

1. Two time-outs during the first half.
2. Three time-outs during the second half with a maximum of two of these time-outs when the game clock shows 2:00 minutes or less in the fourth quarter.
3. One time-out during each overtime.

Inbound the Ball

Whenever the play is stopped due to a violation, foul or ball landed outside the court, the team getting the ball throws it inbounds (restart the play) behind the line of the court nearest to where the violation occurred. When a team scores a basket, the opposing team inbounds the ball from anywhere behind the baseline.

Travelling

A player in possession of the ball must keep one foot intact on the floor, unless he is dribbling, passing or shooting. This foot is usually the first foot that landed on the floor after catching a mid-air ball. It is also a pivot foot.

If landed on both feet at the same time, a player can decide the pivot. If the player moves the pivot foot off the floor, he is not allowed to dribble. He can only pass or shoot the ball before returning the pivot foot back to the ground. Any of these infringement would mean that he has committed a travelling violation.

Double Dribble

A player uses passing or dribbling skills to advance the ball forward for attack. If he dribbles the ball and picks it up with both hands (or at any point of time while dribbling, the ball rest is seen rested on the hand), he is not allowed to dribble the ball again beside passing or shooting. Otherwise, a violation called "double dribble" will be imposed against him and opposition takes the ball from the nearest side or baseline and change possession.

Back Court

The offensive team has to advance the ball to the front court (attacking end) and attempts to make a shot within 24 seconds of the shot clock. Once the ball is past the half-way line to the front court, it cannot be passed back to defensive end (back court), otherwise, the team is said to have violated the "back court" rule, resulting in a change of possession at the side line nearer to where the violation is committed.

The Basic Rules 19

Officiating (Taken from www.fiba.com)

Game clock signals

Scoring

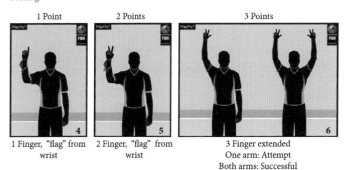

Substitution and Time-out

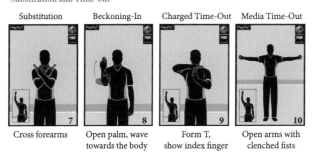

20 *Basketball: A Guide for Physical Education Teachers*

Informative

Cancel Score, Cancel Play

Scissor-like action with arms, once across chest

Visible Count

Counting while moving the palm

Violations

Travelling

Rotate fists

Illegal Dribble: Double Dribbling

Patting motion with palm

Illegal Dribble: Carrying The Ball

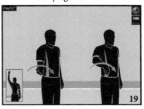

Half rotation with palm

Shot Clock Reset

Rotate hand, extend index finger

Direction Of Play And/Or Out-Of-Bounds

Point in direction of play, arm parallel to sidelines

Held Ball/Jump Ball Situation

Thumbs up, then point in direction of play using the alternating possession arrow

The Basic Rules 21

3 Seconds

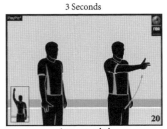

Arm extended,
show 3 fingers

5 Seconds

Show 5 fingers

8 Seconds

Show 8 fingers

24 Seconds

Fingers touch shoulder

Ball Returned To Backcourt

Wave arm front of body

Deliberate Foot Ball

Point to the foot

CHAPTER FIVE
Teaching/Coaching Approaches

Traditional and Games Approach

There are generally two different approaches in teaching basketball, namely the traditional approach and the game concept approach. The traditional approach has been referred to as a technical approach and is characterised by learning through isolated drills and de-contextualised practices. The game concept approach, on the other hand, focuses on teaching games through a conceptually driven approach (through concepts, tactics, and strategies). Usually, the "game concepts" is usually taught through small-sided (situational) games, whereby in a typical lesson, pupils will be given the opportunity to play a game at the beginning as well as at the end of instruction (Griffin *et al.*, 1997). Skills are not neglected in the game concept approach, but are taught in response to the needs of the open situational game.

Game-Based Approach

Game-based coaching uses a variety of games to teach players a new technique or skill,[1] as opposed to utilising isolated drills. Instead of making players practice drills repeatedly until the skills become automatic, game-based coaching uses games designed specifically for players to pick up the new skill or concept the teacher/coach is trying to teach.

Traditional coaching focuses a lot on using drills for players to learn a new skill. In drills, players practice predetermined patterns of a game by repeating the technique. However, this method of utilising drills may be deemed inefficient as game scenarios are never the same. Players may be able to perfect the drill during trainings, thinking that they have learned the new technique. On the other hand, during competitions, they may find themselves confused as they are unable to apply what they have learnt in the drill.

---

[1] https://teachingmotionoffense.weebly.com/what-is-games-based-coaching.html.

Therefore, drills may not allow players to fully understand the reason why certain moves are made during certain scenarios. Instead players merely go through the motion of completing a drill because their teacher/coach made them do it, failing to understand the real purpose of the drill. In this case, players are mastering the drill instead of really learning the skill teachers/coaches want them to pick up.[2]

Game-based coaching taps on the athletes' interest in a game structure to promote skill development and tactical knowledge. Interest and excitement in playing a game as compared to doing drills become positive motivators for players to take part and endure trainings. This alternative form of coaching acts as it utilises a combination of strategy and skills which are essentials to perform in games. It is similar to the inquiry-based teaching approach whereby students/athletes are introduced to a series of scenarios/questions, and are required to problem-solve and discover solutions, facilitated by their teacher/coach. Their exposure and experience in this process may promote curiosity and motivation in learning.

---

[2] https://coachingtoolbox.net/practice/games-based-approach-coaching-basketball.html.

How does it work?

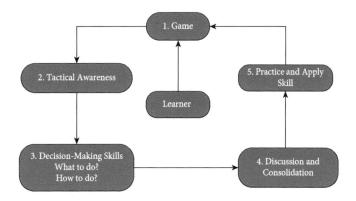

(1) *Game*: The teacher/coach organises respective learning tasks, which focus on developing solutions to tactical problems. They provide players with learning opportunities through specifically designed games that develop tactical awareness and motor skills.

For example, a basketball coach who wishes to teach his players when and how to use a bounce pass can design a half court 5-on-5 game. Players are not allowed to dribble, and they have to make a certain number of consecutive bounce passes before they can score to win the game.

(2) & (3) *Tactical awareness and decision-making skills*: Players are placed in game-like scenarios when executing the game designed by the teacher/coach. This cultivates their tactical awareness and equips

them with better decision-making skills. This is because players are forced to read the game when practicing the skill in an environment that is directly related to a game.

Going back to the bounce pass scenario, players would have to think of how and when to execute bounce passes when a defensive player is guarding them. This cultivates tactical awareness and decision-making skills as players have to think on their feet and read the game.[3]

(4) *Discussion and consolidation*: After playing the game for about 10–15 minutes, the teacher/coach then gathers his players for a question-and-answer session. Teachers/Coaches are primary sources of expertise and they can enhance their players' learning abilities. They can aid their players to consolidate their learning by linking the initial modified game and the skill practice through questioning. The quality of these questions is critical for effective learning. This is also a good time for players to clarify any doubts that they may have.

For example, teachers/coaches can ask questions such as, "What are the advantages of utilising bounce

---

[3] https://teachingmotionoffense.weebly.com/what-is-games-based-coaching.html.

passes as compared to other passes, and when do we use a bounce pass?" This forces players to think back on the skill or technique used, hence ensuring better understanding of what the teacher/coach is trying to put across through the game.

(5) *Practice and apply skill*: Within each training session, players practice skills after they have experienced a game that presents a tactical problem requiring that certain skill. Equipped with better understanding of when and how to use the skill, players are now able to apply what they have learnt in the game. With consistent practice, they are able to master the skill learnt and subsequently transfer the same skill and technique across games.

Advantages

As compared to the traditional way of coaching which focuses heavily on the use of drills, game-based coaching allows players to learn techniques and skills better. This is because game participation is more interesting and motivating than skill development drills. Using a game to teach a skill provides everyone an opportunity to practice what they have learnt. Hence, players are able to better understand the reason why certain moves are made during games, allowing them to apply what they have learnt in future games.

Players are also placed in an environment that is more realistic to games, therefore allowing them to get used to when and how to execute certain moves. Tactical awareness and other types of learning can also be transferred across games.

Tactical awareness largely refers to a basketball player having the ability to make effective decisions during a basketball game.[4] Having tactical awareness is also a prerequisite to performance skill.

Players are better equipped with necessary skills such as tactical awareness and quick decision-making skills. These skills are essential in game plays as players have to react to the different game scenarios and outsmart their opponents in order to win a game.[5] Therefore, better tactical awareness greatly enhances a player's game performance.

Drill-driven coaching only focuses on a player's psychomotor learning. This is because players go through the motion of executing the drills that their teacher/coach wants them to do, without thinking about how and when the skill learnt can be applied during games. Hence, players are unable to transfer what they have learnt in drills across games.

---

[4] https://prezi.com/io45_w2ytxgw/technical-and-tactical-skills-in-sport/.
[5] https://us.humankinetics.com/blogs/excerpt/why-game-play-is-just-as-important-as-a-tactical-approach.

In comparison, game-based coaching taps on all three domains of learning. It improves a player's cognitive, affective, and psychomotor learning. When using a game to teach a game, players are placed in game scenarios, forcing them to solve a given problem utilising the cognitive domain. This then facilitates performance in the psychomotor domain.

Positive benefits and outcomes have been associated with using a game-based approach on pupils' learning during physical education lessons (Launder, 2001). However, in terms of skills and knowledge, there were no differences between the traditional approach and the game concept approach (e.g., Wright *et al.*, 2005).

The games approach in action:

1. select modified (situational) game,
2. observe and assess players at play,
3. ask questions,
4. teach, practice, and refine skills and tactics,
5. back to situational game.

Alternatively, the teacher/coach can also use the IDEA approach if a traditional approach is preferred.

IDEA skill instruction:

1. introduce the skill,
2. demonstrate the skill,

3. explain the skill,
4. attend to players practicing the skills.

Modifying Games

There are a few elements for modifying the game in order to highlight certain "game scenarios" or to cater for different abilities and better engage them in learning. The key is to build learners' confidence levels and enhance their competence in applying the skill learned in a less complication/demanding game situation. Teachers or coaches can consider the following elements:

1. change court size,
2. use lopsided games,
3. change rules,
4. shorten length of game,
5. adjust defensive pressure.

Some Examples of Modified Games

Passing game

1. players to play 4 on 2 then 3 on 3 on a half court (allows higher success rate initially),
2. two passes before shooting,
3. determine type of passes used during game,
4. no dribbling is allowed.

Give and go

1. players to play 4 on 2 then 3 on 3 on a half court (allows higher success rate initially),
2. two passes before shooting,
3. shots within five feet,
4. start off with no dribbling,
5. dribble to score or pass to teammate to score (dribble with a purpose).

Screens

1. players to play 4 on 2 then 3 on 3 on a half court (allows higher success rate initially),
2. points awarded for basket off a screen.

Player to player

1. players to play 4 on 4 on a half court,
2. defence calls and execute switches,
3. pick and roll.

Layups

1. players to play 3 on 1 on a half court,
2. defender in the lane,
3. no dribbling except while drive in for layups.

Fast break

1. players to play 3 on 2, or 2 on 1 on a half court,
2. transit to 3 on 2 and 2 on 1 on a full court,
3. off-court player to join in for fast breaks by rotation.

CHAPTER SIX
Suggested Teaching/ Coaching Sequences

In terms of teaching/coaching basic skills in basketball, we recommend teachers/coaches to start with the following sequence. However, it does not mean that teachers have to teach these skills one at a time. It can be a mixed and match type of lesson whereby within a lesson, several skills are taught with appropriate progression. For example, there can be components on footwork, fitness and conditioning, passing and receiving, shooting and layups within one lesson. In this way, lessons have lots of variety and students' interest will be kept high throughout each lesson.

Ball Handling

Ball handling is an essential activity that every student should learn prior to the other skills or technique. It helps the student to have a good "feel" of the ball without looking at it and eventually have a better control of the ball during play. That is what she/he needs to do in order to enjoy the game.

Teaching Points:

1. head and eyes look up,
2. use fingers instead of palm,
3. maintain a balanced stance,
4. increase speed of execution.

Common Mistake	Consequence	Remediation
Using palms.	No control of the ball.	Use paddings of fingers only.
Looking down at the ball.	Cannot see what is in front or ahead of him/her.	Keep head and eyes up, look in front.
Straight legs, knees not bent.	Results in less or no control of the ball.	Balanced stance, feet shoulder width apart. Wider stance if necessary.

Organisation (assuming a class size of 40 students, with 20 basketballs and 1 standard basketball court):

Suggested Teaching/Coaching Sequences 37

1. In pairs, one ball between two players.
2. One student performs each of the following activities at one side of the court while his/her partner jogs from sideline to sideline to avoid waiting time.
3. Teacher/coach decides on the number of activities per lesson and varies the tasks to suit the different abilities of the players.

Figure of 8 Leg No Dribble (see below figure):

1. feet wide apart,
2. ball is moved in a "figure 8" action,
3. around the legs,
4. change direction of the ball's movement,
5. count the number of successful catch within a time limit.

38 *Basketball: A Guide for Physical Education Teachers*

Figure of 8 Leg Dribble (see below figure):

1. dribble the ball in a "figure of 8" action,
2. around the legs,
3. change direction,
4. count the number of successful dribbles,
5. complete within a time limit.

Straddle Flip (see below figure):

1. feet wide apart,
2. hold the ball with both hands in front,
3. between the legs,
4. flip the ball into the air and catch the ball again,
5. with two hands behind the legs before it hits the ground,
6. count the number of successful catches within a time limit.

Variation 1 (see below figure):

1. start with holding the ball between the legs,
2. flip the ball into the air and catch the ball again by alternating the hands before the ball hits the ground,
3. count the number of successful catch within a time limit.

40 *Basketball: A Guide for Physical Education Teachers*

Waist Wrap (see below figure):

1. hold the ball in one hand, take it around your waist and pass it to the other hand in one continuous motion,
2. pass the ball around the waist in either direction.

Variation 2 (see below figure):

1. pass the ball around the head, waist and below the knees,

2. repeat the same cycle from below the knees waist and back to head level,
3. count the number of cycle completed within a time limit.

Double Leg–Single Leg (see below figure):

1. start with feet together,
2. rotate the ball around both legs,
3. step sideward with one leg and rotate the ball around that leg,
4. bring the feet together and rotate the ball around both feet,
5. side step to opposite direction, rotate the ball around that leg,
6. bring the feet together and rotate the ball around them,
7. repeat the same sequence and count the number of successful catch within a time limit.

Fun Activities:

1. individual or pairs to compete with each other by executing each activity with speed,
2. get students to think about ball handing moves that have not been covered in the lessons and get them to demonstrate to the class. This promotes creativity among the students.

In 2's, compete with another group. Student with the ball will initiate the ball handling drills and one student from the other group will try to follow. The partner from both groups will jog from sideline to sideline while this is happening. Change over the role after those students who have finished jogging from sideline to sideline once.

Basic Individual Offensive Skills

The development of a basketball player's individual offence is very important. A player with excellent offensive skills makes the job of the defender difficult. Therefore, emphasis should be placed on teaching fundamental offensive skills to the young players.

Footwork

Offensive Footwork:

1. it is used to outdo the defender during offence,
2. effective offensive footwork aims to gain the initiative and half a pace on opponent in order gain advantage.

Teaching Points:

1. balance body, bend knees,
2. keep body low,
3. use flat feet,
4. change of pace, especially when dribbling,
5. change of direction when closely marked,
6. change of direction and pace for eluding and cutting behind a defender.

Types of Stop:

1. stride stop: 1–2 rhythm,
2. jump stop: (2 feet land at the same time).

Common Mistake	Consequence	Remediation
Knees are not bent at the correct angle.	Unstable and slow in movement.	Keep knees bent at 100 to 110 degree.
Not pushing hard enough on opposite foot.	Slow in movement.	Keep body low, place weight on opposite foot (left) and push off hard toward opposite direction to shake off opponent.

Organisation:

1. in pairs and find a space for passing.

Suggested Activities:

1. one player to pass the ball to another player,
2. receiver aims to receive the ball half a body length in front of the passer,
3. change role.

Variation:

1. partner can vary the pace and directions to make the task more challenging.

Pivoting

It is an essential footwork in offence and to protect the ball. In offence, pivoting can help the player gain space for attacking the basket.

Teaching Points (Simple and reverse pivot):

1. pivot on ball of foot,
2. pivoting foot must keep in contact with floor,
3. keep head and eyes up,
4. knee bent and keep body low,
5. keep ball away from the opponent/close to body.

Common Mistake	Consequence	Remediation
Pivot using the whole/flat foot.	Slow in movement. Body is unstable.	Pivot using ball of the foot, heel up.
Knees are not bent at the correct angle.	Unstable and slow in movement.	Keep knees bent at 100 to 110 degree.
Head is looking down.	Unsure where is the opponent.	Look at opponent up/head up.

Organisation:

1. individual. Find a space for footwork.

Suggested Activities:

1. jog around, upon hearing whistle (by the teacher/coach), adopt jump stop position (land with both feet at the same time), pivots in clockwise direction using dominant foot. Continue jogging upon completion of task.

Variation:

1. change the pivot foot,
2. change in directions,
3. in pairs, jog behind partner,
4. upon hearing the whistle, both do a jump stop, followed by a pivot, and change role,
5. chase partner instead of jogging behind partner,
6. use the same arrangement for pivoting and role play.

Passing and receiving

Passing

Chest pass:

Chest pass is usually used for quick and straight pass to maintain possession or to advance the ball forward.

Teaching Points:

1. fingers relaxed and spread over the ball,
2. thumbs behind the ball,
3. step forward on the release,
4. finish with thumbs pointing to the ground and fingers pointing to the target,
5. the receiver should catch the ball at his/her chest level.

Suggested Teaching/Coaching Sequences **47**

Bounce pass

Teaching Points:

1. same as chest pass except finishes with thumbs and fingers pointing to the ground,
2. aim and bounce the ball at two-thirds the distance to receiver,
3. the receiver should catch the ball at his/her waist level.

Overhead pass

Usually used for a long distance or over a defender
Teaching Points:

1. ball is held with paddings of fingers and upper portion of palm above the forehead,
2. step towards receiver,
3. snap wrist to follow through,
4. receiver should still receive the ball at chest height.

Common Mistake	Consequence	Remediation
Chest Pass No control over the ball.	Ball could not reach the desired target.	Spread fingers around the ball. Step forward when making a pass.
Did not straighten the elbows.	Speed of the ball is slow.	Extend elbows. Fingers point at target after ball released.
Bounce Pass The bouncing distance between the thrower and receiver is incorrect.	Ball could not reach the desired target.	Spread fingers around the ball. Push ball downward with extended elbows.
Did not straighten the elbows.		Bounce ball (fingers pointing) at the distance 2/3 to the receiver.

(Continued)

Common Mistake	Consequence	Remediation
Overhead Pass		
Ball travels too low.	Could not clear the defender.	Ball is held above forehead.
	Ball takes longer time to reach the receiver.	Snap wrist to follow through.
Ball travels in a loop manner.	Higher chance of interception by the defender.	Ball travels straight (high to low) line manner.

Receiving

Teaching Points:

1. hands at chest level and spread out fingers,
2. watch and catch the ball into the hands,
3. hold the ball firmly upon catching.

50 *Basketball: A Guide for Physical Education Teachers*

Organisations:

1. in pairs, one ball between two players,
2. passer to perform one type of pass,
3. receiver receives the ball in a triple threat position,
4. take turns to be passer and receiver,
5. teacher decides on the number of passes made for each task,
6. teacher decides on the type of passes for each task.

Variation 1:

1. alternate the type of passes, for example, player 1 makes a chest pass to player 2, player 2 returns with a bounce pass to player 1 (see figure),
2. pass ball from a stationary position to passing on the move,
3. pass or receive ball at the designated cone/marker.

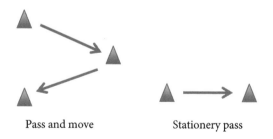

Pass and move   Stationery pass

Variation 2: 3 V 1 Monkey Game

1. teacher decides on the type of passes to be used for the game. Start off with using one type of pass

first. Include other type of passes when players are more proficient with each type of pass,
2. players can only pass or receive at the cone/marker to reinforce skill learned and the ability to transfer in a modified game situation,
3. if the passer committed a "turnover" (missed pass), he shall take over the "monkey".

Variation 3:

1. three basketballs per team,
2. every player holds on to a basketball,
3. player on the left and right lanes (number 1 and 3) uses bounce pass whilst middle player 2 (number 1) uses chest pass (refer to the following figure) while they advance the ball forward,
4. change position/group upon reaching the baseline of other side of the court.

Variation 4:

1. proceed to 3 V 2 and 3 V 3 game eventually,
2. groups nearer to the baskets use the normal scoring method while those at the centre court could score at the sidelines (see the following figure),
3. manipulate the rules, e.g., type of pass, time allowed hold on to the ball etc. to simulate game-like situations.

52 *Basketball: A Guide for Physical Education Teachers*

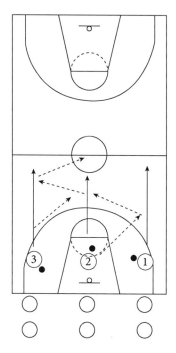

Drills for improving passing

Parallel line drill

The ball is passed between the players as indicated with the dotted lines in the diagram.

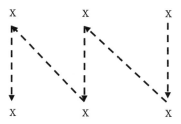

Pepper pot drill

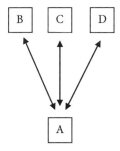

1. see diagram, at least two balls used,
2. players B and C each holds on to a ball,
3. B passes ball to A and A passes the ball to D,
4. C passes to A and A passes the ball to B.

Shooting

Scoring baskets is the ultimate objective in basketball. The team that scored more baskets wins the game. However, shooting is a refined skill that needs correct techniques and with lots of practice. When teaching, the emphasis should be on developing good shooting habits rather than scoring.

The following steps are good for teaching the correct techniques, and will help teachers to "break down" the shooting for the ease of diagnosis and intervention.

Set shot

Teaching Points:

1. feet shoulder width apart,
2. bend knees to achieve a good balance,
3. shooting hand foot slightly in front of the other and pointing towards the basket,
4. arms — shooting arm in "L" shape under ball, non-shooting hand at the side of the basketball,
5. angles (bend elbow at 90 degrees) and with ball just above forehead,
6. bend the wrist far back to see the wrinkles at the wrist, spread the fingers,
7. ball should touch the fingertips and not the palm, push ball up from the legs and straighten the arm with elbow locked,
8. snap the wrist for the follow through.

The non-shooting hand should be on the side of the basketball.

The following acronym — BEEF can be used to help students learn and remember set shot better:

B – Balance
E – Elbow
E – Elevation or Eyes (on the target)
F – Follow-through

Suggested Teaching/Coaching Sequences 55

Common Mistake	Consequence	Remediation
Hands Position Using palm to hold/shoot the ball.	No control of the ball. Ball could not reach the desired direction.	Ball rests on the fingers rather than palm. Non-shooting hand is at the side of the ball rather than in front/at the back of the ball.

(*Continued*)

(*Continued*)

Common Mistake	Consequence	Remediation
Aiming Inconsistent aiming.	Cannot get the ball into the ring. Inconsistent shots.	Feet shoulder width apart. Align index finger or elbow with the centre part of the ring.
Shooting Using upper body strength (e.g. fingers, hands) rather than bigger muscles groups to transfer force.	Ball cannot reach the ring.	Bent knees to 90 or 100 degree to activate the bigger muscles for strength and power. Hold ball at the waist level. Straighten the knees; bring the ball up above the forehead.
Ball hitting front part of the ring (wrong trajectory).	Cannot get the ball into the basket. Ball is touching the front part of the basket ring.	Release the ball in an upward and forward manner. Extend the elbow and follow through with palm facing down. Release the ball high in an upward and forward manner. Follow through with extended elbow and palm facing down.

Suggested Activities:

1. one ball between two players. Practice shooting technique with partner. Observe and give feedback to each other,
2. progress to one player shoots and partner retrieve ball activity. Emphasise on quick shot and good passing timing,
3. four players in a group, first player of each group practices set shot for 10 times while the other three teammates help to retrieve and pass the ball back to the shooter. Rotate the role after 10 shots,
4. rotate the shooting position upon the completion of two rounds of practice,
5. the middle court can be used for skills/concepts revision or modified games, e.g. 3 V 3 game,
6. rotate the groups at different play areas after designated time.

Variation 1:

Baseline: Both shooters spin ball to mid post. They land with a jump stop with feet facing the other basket. They then execute a forward pivot, shoot then rebound the ball before going to other baseline. Allow sufficient time to work on forward pivot before changing drill so players are shooting off a reverse pivot. Other groups can work from the space from the centre court. Players to execute pivot step with a set shot, allow ball to land and bounce on the ground once before picking up the ball and join back the group. Change over groups when targets have been met or reached designated time.

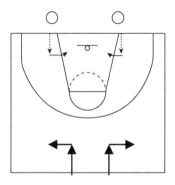

Variation 2:

Shooting competition: Same group as previous activity in this lesson. All groups start shooting concurrently. The first group to score six baskets will shout "change" and quickly move to the next shooting spot in a clockwise direction manner. The group rotate within the half court. This activity emphasises quick and good shooting technique with accurate passing skill. Refer to below diagram.

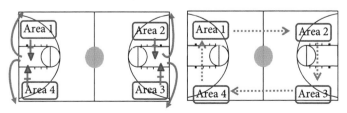

Suggested Teaching/Coaching Sequences 59

Variation 3: Two on One Drill

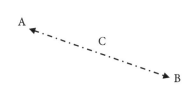

1. the thrower (A or B) is allowed to take one step in any direction prior to making the pass,
2. the defender in the middle (C) is to intercept the pass,
3. manipulate the rules such as the types of passes can be used or movement of the receiver or passer to make the tasks more challenging.

Variation 4: Bull in the *Ring*

1. the players (x) line up as per diagram,
2. the ball is to be kept continually on the move, the person in the centre A will attempt to intercept the ball,
3. the ball must not be passed to immediate neighbour.

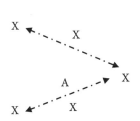

60 *Basketball: A Guide for Physical Education Teachers*

Variation 5: Four corners passing and cutting

1. four corners with four balls,
2. the front person at each line passes the ball to the second person in the opposite file in an anticlockwise direction,
3. after the pass, he runs to join the file to which he has passed the ball.

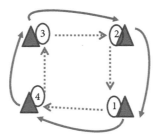

Variation 6: Circle *passing*

1. the players line up as per diagram,
2. the ball can be passed to any person in the circle except to immediate neighbour,
3. use one or two balls.

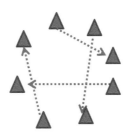

Dribbling

Dribbling should only be used when a pass is not possible. Player should continue to dribble until there is a passing or scoring opportunity. To start dribbling, the ball must contact the floor before lifting the pivot foot.

Teaching Points:

1. head and eyes up, not on the basketball,
2. use paddings of fingers and upper portion of palm,
3. protect the ball with the body,
4. dribble with purpose,
5. exposure to dribbling with the right or left hands,
6. vary the speed of dribbling to make the offence unpredictable.

Control dribble — left and right hands

Teaching Points:

1. use paddings of fingers and upper palm for control,
2. push ball downward with spread fingers and elbow extended,
3. bend knees and dribble ball at about waist height,
4. head up, eyes up looking forward,
5. alternate right hand and left hand.

Protection dribble

Teaching Points:

1. keep the body between the ball and the defender,
2. maintain a low stance by bending the knees (90 to 100 degree),
3. protect ball with lead foot and arm,
4. use "big to bigger" footwork and do not bring the feet together.

Crossover dribble

Teaching Points:

1. push off the foot (same as the dribble hand) when changing direction,
2. change hands with a low (knee height) controlled dribble,

Suggested Teaching/Coaching Sequences **63**

3. non-dribbling hand held close to pick up the ball on crossover,
4. head up and eyes looking forward,
5. bend knees with feet shoulder width apart for balance.

Speed dribble

Teaching Points:

1. push ball forward (one arm distance) and chase with elbow extended,
2. keep the ball in front and to the side of the body,
3. dribble with paddings of fingers and upper portion of palm,
4. head and eyes up,
5. quick first step by pushing off the ball of the foot,
6. maintain control by keeping the ball at waist level,
7. dribble with alternating hands for maximum speed.

Behind the back dribble

Teaching Points:

1. head and eyes up,
2. sharp change of direction,
3. bring ball behind the back with control (extended elbow and fingers spread),
4. change pace and bounce ball next to opposite foot,
5. dribble with the other hand and push ball forward.

Suggested Teaching/Coaching Sequences **65**

Between the legs

Teaching Points:

1. head and eyes up,
2. come to a stop with spread feet,
3. stay low and balanced,

4. push ball downward, bouncing between the middle of the legs change pace and use body to shield the ball.

Common Mistake	Consequence	Remediation
Controlled/Protection dribble		
No control over the ball.	Ball could not reach the desired direction.	Spread fingers around the ball.
Did not extend elbow.		Push the ball downward by extending the elbow.
Look at the ball. No spatial awareness.	Unable to have a good vision to read the game, especially on the defenders.	Head and eyes up.
Speed dribble		
Taking too many bounces/dribbles to the desired distance.	Unable to pass the defender.	Head and eyes up. Push the ball forward by extending the elbow.
Bounce ball too close to the body.		Chase for the ball.
Crossover dribble		
Did not use shoulders/body to protect the ball.	The ball is "open" to the opponent.	Shoulder and leg crossed at the same time, e.g. when the ball is crossed over from right hand to left

Suggested Teaching/Coaching Sequences 67

(*Continued*)

Common Mistake	Consequence	Remediation
		hand, the right shoulder and right left should follow to protect the ball. Cross the ball about one arm distance in front of the defender. Keep body low by bending knees.
Cross the ball too far away from the defender.	Not able to dribble pass the defender.	Crossover the ball and use shoulder and arm to shield the ball, e.g. dribble with right hand, when crossed the ball to left hand, right shoulder and leg should follow-up through so that the ball is shield.
Behind the back		
No control of the ball.	Cannot control the ball.	Keep body low by bending knees.
Hand and angle of the ball is incorrect.	The ball is far away from the body and is not shielded.	Hand and eyes up. Extend the execution hand all the way behind the back. Control the ball with fingers spread.

(*Continued*)

(Continued)

Common Mistake	Consequence	Remediation
		Push and direct the ball close to the other side of the body. Free hand protects the ball and accelerates the ball forward.
Between the legs Feet too closed to each other.	No control over the ball. Not enough space to dribble the ball between the legs.	Stay low and bend knees. Feet shoulder width apart for balance. Bounce ball fast in between the legs using spread fingers.
Dribble too far from the defender.	Could not clear the defender despite crossing the ball.	Dribble the ball about one arm distance in front of the defender. Head and eyes up. Accelerate after dribble has been executed.

Organisation:

1. in pairs, one ball between two players.

Activities:

1. a dribbles and looks at B's hands at the same time and shout out the number loud. When 1 reaches the side line of the court, player changes over role. See the following diagram.

Suggested Teaching/Coaching Sequences **69**

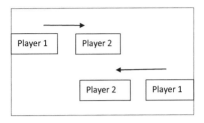

Variation 1:

Dribble chase: Three to four players per group. Players are to dribble and chase after the others. To stay in the game, they have to "touch" another player while maintain the dribble, at the same time, avoid being touched by other players. Once a player is touched by other, he will be out of the game.

Attack Dribble: players 1, 2 and 3 dribble off from the 3-point line while players 4, 5 and 6 dribble off from the baseline. When meeting in the middle, they "read" the opponent and dribble away. Refer to the following diagram.

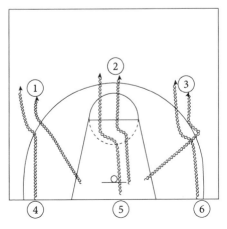

Teacher/coach decides on the type of dribbling skills to be used for each activity.

The Layup

The layup is the highest percentage shot in basketball and once mastered; it is the easiest shot in basketball. However, it can also be the hardest skill to teach due to the complexity of movements involved. Emphasis must be on correct footwork and the ability to shoot the layup with both the right and left hand.

Points to Consider:

1. use "set shot" technique,
2. pick the ball up with two hands,
3. jump off inside foot and bring opposite knee up,
4. non-shooting arm protects shot,
5. eyes on target,
6. release ball high off the backboard softly.

Suggested Teaching/Coaching Sequences 71

Common Mistake	Consequence	Remediation
Footwork Wrong take off foot/step.	Lack of height. Ball is not shielded. Not balanced.	Catch the ball next to the opposite foot. Push off the left foot for a right hand layup (i.e. stop the ball with left foot, take a step and push off with left foot again). Stay low and push hard when takeoff. Lift right foot and right arm (shooting arm) up. Ball ahead of forehead in a

(*Continued*)

(*Continued*)

Common Mistake	Consequence	Remediation
		ready to shoot (set shot) position. Eyes on the basketball board and release the ball softly.
Aiming Incorrect aiming. Release the ball too hard against the basketball board.	Cannot get the ball into the basket. Ball bounce off the board.	Get the ball to the top right hand corner of the rectangular box. Bring the ball above forehead at the highest point after takeoff. Follow through with palm and fingers pointing down.

Suggested Progression:

1. *two steps layup*: same arrangement as the previous activity (stop the ball with left foot forward for right handed), students take additional two steps and shout "right-left-layup" at the same time. Retrieve own rebound, pass the ball to teammate and join the queue,
2. move back slightly away from the board. Take one bounce; stop the ball, and execute a two-step count layup,

3. increase the distance and allow more bounces (dribbles) to be taken before executing a two-step count layup,
4. self-toss, catch the ball, and execute a layup,
5. two rows, one player passes the ball by tossing in front of the shooter, the shooter catch the ball and execute a layup. Feeder follow the shooter to get the rebound, dribble the ball at the sideline and join the shooter queue, and vice versa.

Variation:

1. in a group of 4's, first player from each group execute a layup shot (push and layup within dribbling). Push off the left foot if using right hand to layup. Retrieve own rebound, pass the ball to his/her teammate, and join queue,
2. each group to complete x number of successful shots before switching over to the other side of the basketball board,
3. the middle portion of the court can be used to revise game concepts or practice individual skills that the students have learned before. Set time for them to switch over with the others who are practising layup drill,
4. play game using layups to score.

Movements without ball

The basic ingredient for all the cuts (offensive moves) is sudden and quick change of direction. The cuts can be executed at any parts of the court.

Straight cut

It is a quick break out from the defender in a straight line (refer to the following figure).

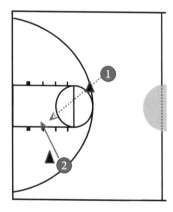

Teaching Points:

1. stay low, bent knees,
2. push off the foot opposite the direction of attack,
3. body weight on the ball of the foot (push off foot),
4. signal hand (away from the defender) to receive ball,
5. square body to face the basket upon receiving ball,

6. assume triple threat position (a position where player has the options to pass, shoot, or dribble).

Organisation:

1. in pairs, one ball between the 2's,
2. one student performs the straight cut, partner times the cut and passes the ball to the cutter at the appropriate time,
3. teacher/coach decides on the number of passes/cuts or time spent on this activity.

Variation 1: To emphasis accurate pass and good timing for each pass.

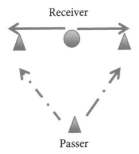

1. passer stations at one cone,
2. receiver/ cutter moves/cuts from one cone to the other (refer to diagram),
3. the pass must be sent to the designated cone,
4. change over the role based on number of successful passes or by timing.

Variation 2:

1. add a defender,
2. attacker goes 1 on 1, attacking the basket.

Common Mistake	Consequence	Remediation
Did not push off the foot fast enough.	Slow in getting off the defender.	Stay low, weight on ball of the foot.
Did not communicate with the passer.	Unable to receive the ball with the right timing.	Signal hand to receive ball.
Body faces away from the basket.	Can only pass to teammate.	Assume triple threats position by pivoting and squaring body to face the basket.

Backdoor cut

A backdoor cut is an offensive manoeuvre that involves a player without the ball moving towards the basket behind the defence in an attempt to receive a pass.

This technique is useful when the defender is heavily marking the lead on the wing. It is the first part of the "V" cut that involves reading the situation, establishing good position, and making eye contact with the player with the ball (refer to the following figure).

Teaching Points:

1. be patient and move deliberately, do not overreact to the defender,
2. if the defenders move out past the 3-point line,
3. offender should execute backdoor cut,
4. the offender should "fake" by pushing off on the foot closest to sideline and step with the foot closest to the basket,
5. passer should time the pass and ensure that the offensive player receives the ball inside key area with either a chest or bounce pass.

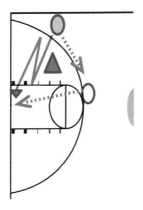

Organisation:

1. same as the straight cut.

Common Mistake	Consequence	Remediation
Did not fake and push off the pivot foot fast enough.	Slow in getting off the defender.	Stay low, weight on ball of the foot.
Did not communicate with the passer.	Unable to receive the ball will the right timing.	Signal hand to receive ball.

Movements with ball

This technique provides another option for attacking when the passing option is not available. The following moves are always performed from the triple threat position.

Jab step and drive

The jab step is also known as "1/2" step "fake drive" made with the non-pivot foot. This can be done in two ways: (a) drive towards the same direction of the fake or (b) crossover to the opposite side of the fake and drive towards the basket for a layup shot.

Teaching Points:

1. execute the jab step and observe the defender,
2. if the defender does not react, the offender extends this step and drive towards the basketball, otherwise, change the direction of the jab (crossover) and dribble towards the basket.

Suggested Teaching/Coaching Sequences 79

Organisation:

1. in pair, one ball between 2 players,
2. attacker performs the jab step and drive move, defender adopts passive defence,
3. the attacker drives pass the defender and stop after driving pass defender,
4. defender move forward and takes up the defensive position again,
5. repeat the same sequence from sideline to sideline,
6. change over the role.

Variation 1:

1. 6 groups — 2 groups practice jab step and drive to the basket while the other 4 groups practice jab step from one end of the sideline to the end of the court,
2. rotate the groups according to time given.

Common Mistake	Consequence	Remediation
Taking too big a step, and off balanced.	Slow in executing quick fake and dribbling pass the defender.	Take half step on the non-pivot foot. Stay low, push off with the pivot foot when driving for a layup.
Ball not protected.	Offender intercepted the ball.	Place ball at the side of the waist/hip level away from the defender. Shield ball with shoulders and free hand/arm.

Jab step and shoot

This technique is useful when the defender has stepped back during the jab step and created a "space/distance" which allows the offender to take a clear shot.

Organisation:

1. same as the jab step and drive activity.

Teaching Points:

1. execute the jab step and observe the defender,
2. if the defender commits to the jab step, offender retreats the step and shoot the ball.

Common Mistake	Consequence	Remediation
Taking too big a step, and off balanced.	Slow in pulling back the step for a quick and clear shot.	Take half step on the non-pivot foot. Stay low, weight on the pivot foot when pulling back the jab step for taking a shot.

(Continued)

(Continued)

Common Mistake	Consequence	Remediation
Ball not being protected.	Offender intercepted the ball.	Place ball at the side of the waist/hip level away from the defender. Shield ball with shoulders and free hand/arm.

Shot fake and drive

This technique involves bringing the ball up into shooting position (eyes on the basket) to fake the defender for a layup shot.

Teaching Points:

1. execute fake shot and observe the defender,
2. if the defender jumps or reaches up to get a hand to the shot, the offender should drive pass the left of right side of the defender using "side step" or "crossover step" and go for a layup shot,
3. the ball is kept at the side (away from the defender) when dribbling.

Suggested Teaching/Coaching Sequences 83

Common Mistake	Consequence	Remediation
The fake shot action is weak: ball is not held high or fast enough for the shooting option.	Offender remains unmoved and no dribbling options are available.	Eyes on the basket. Bring the ball high above the forehead with quick action.
Lower body position not adopted. Did not bend the knees.	Unable to generate power for a quick a shot.	Knees bent, body weight on the feet.

Shot fake and shoot

This technique requires creating a fake shot to draw the defender to react. Look for shooting opportunity when the defender is off-guarded or balanced.

 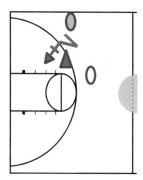

Teaching Points:

1. execute fake shot and observe the defender,
2. if the defender does not react to the shot fake, the offender shoots the ball immediately.

Suggested Teaching/Coaching Sequences 85

Common Mistake	Consequence	Remediation
Making too many fake shots in a slow moment.	Offender remains unmoved and no shooting option is available.	Eyes on the basket. Fake once or twice and be ready to take quick shot. Shoot the ball immediately when the defender is not reacting to the fake shot.
Lower body position not adopted. Did not bend knees.	Unable to generate power for a quick a shot.	Knees bent, body weight on the feet.

Rebounding

It is used to increase opportunities to attack the basket.

Teaching Points:

1. try to gain inside position (e.g., use fake, change of direction),
2. be aggressive,
3. time your jump and catch ball at its highest point,
4. once you have the ball, shield it and look for shot, or pass out; a fake and shot is particularly useful.

Basic Individual Defensive Skills

This section focuses on basic individual defensive skills. Some of the key skills are:

Basic stance and footwork

In Basketball, the basic defensive stance is called a Boxer's stance. This is effective for countering opponent's offence.

Teaching Points:

1. place weight on the balls of your feet, feet shoulder width apart,
2. balanced: knees bent, back straight,
3. place arms out with your palms up and elbows bent a little,
4. move directional foot first then recover other foot,
5. focus on your opponent's mid-section.

Common Mistake	Consequence	Remediation
Body weight on both feet. Feet are more or less than shoulder width.	Reaction time will be slower. Body unstable.	Weight on the balls of the feet. Feet shoulder width apart.
Knees are bent at the 90 degree angle.	Unstable and slow in movement.	Keep knees bent at 100 to 110 degree.
Directional foot is not pointing at the direction of move.	Unstable and slow in movement.	Point leading foot towards the direction of move.

(*Continued*)

(*Continued*)

Common Mistake	Consequence	Remediation
Crossed feet.	Unstable in body movement.	Move directional foot first and bring in the other foot without crossing over.

Defensive footwork is a quick defensive method to keep up with opponent.

Teaching Points:

1. feet shoulder width apart,
2. body weight on the balls of the feet,
3. knees bent, back straight,
4. head up to look in front,
5. position arms to pressure the opponent from dribbling or shooting,
6. leading foot points towards the direction of move,
7. push off with the trail foot and take "big step" with the leading foot,
8. do not cross feet, maintain balanced.

Common Mistake	Consequence	Remediation
Did not bend knees or body is not low enough.	Slow in defensive moment.	Eyes on the basket. Feet shoulder width apart. Bend knees. Shoot ball immediately when the defender is not reacting to the fake shot.
Jumping instead of sliding the step/foot.	Body off balanced.	Take big step on the leading foot. Toe points at the direction of movement.
Arms not raised.	Opponents are able to dribble or shoot.	Position arms (one up and one to the side) to prevent attacker from dribbling and shooting.

Organisation:

1. in pairs and find space.

Suggested Activities:

1. "mirror" your partner,
2. move in different directions (left and right),
3. check each other's stance,

4. change role when the stance is not properly executed or time set by teacher.

Variation:

1. "mirror" partner but in different directions,
2. vary the directions (e.g. left, right, diagonal etc.),
3. have a "leader" to lead a group (e.g. 6–8 players) using the above mentioned activities.

Basic arm action

It is a basic defensive action to stop attacking player from getting easy ball and counter attack.

Teaching Points (Defensive):

1. use same arm as foot when advance forward,
2. enlarge the area of obstacle to pass, shoot or dribble,
3. "lead" opponent by allowing only one avenue of movement which you are ready to close,
4. one arm attacking ball, other arm low and covering approach to basket or centre of court,
5. be ready for quick change of arm positions.

Drop step

It is generally used for a change of direction.

Suggested Teaching/Coaching Sequences **91**

Teaching Points:

1. take short and sharp steps,
2. maintain good balance,
3. keep stance shoulder width apart.

Common Mistake	Consequence	Remediation
Slow in executing drop step.	Unable to contain the opponent.	Keep body low and balanced. Feet shoulder width. Take short and sharp step.

92 *Basketball: A Guide for Physical Education Teachers*

Organisation:

1. adopt defensive stance and slide from one end of the sideline to the other end using left foot to lead,
2. repeat in the opposite direction using the right foot to lead.

Variation 1: Keeping head up and quick reaction time

1. all students facing the teacher (as shown in the figure),
2. teacher uses hands to signal direction of move. Students follow the direction of movement,
3. slide towards the opposite direction of the teacher,
4. vary the directions (e.g. left, right, front, and back) and quickness (e.g. fast and slow).

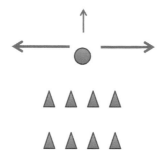

Variation 2:

1. one ball between two players,

2. attacker dribbles from sideline to sideline, defender uses the proper footwork to defend — keeping one arm distance away from the attacker,
3. defender stays half a body length ahead of the attacker, keep body low and places body weight on the ball of the feet,
4. attacker can change direction of the dribble to work the defender harder.

Variation 3:
Combine the offensive moves learnt in the previous lessons, for example, execute jab step and shoot in a 1V1 modified game. The focus of the game will be both on defensive and offensive movements.

Blocking out

Blocking out is a technique to minimise opponent for getting a second chance/opportunity to score.

Teaching Points:

1. sag off opponent when shot is taken,
2. watch your opponent, not the ball,
3. cut off his line to basket by pivoting (get him behind you),
4. catch the ball at its highest point (straighten knees and elbows extended),

5. be aggressive, and do not fear of body contact,
6. shield the ball with body and arms upon receiving the ball,
7. catch the rebound firmly.

Common Mistake	Consequence	Remediation
Go for the ball instead of blocking out opponent after a shot has been taken.	Unable to block out and keep opponent away behind one's back.	Look at where the opponent is running towards the basketball. Step towards the opponent, pivot and keep him/her at the back. Look at the board and go for the ball.

Basic Offensive Team Tactics

Basic floor spacing

One of the common mistakes made by players is following the ball, resulting in crowding around the ball

Suggested Teaching/Coaching Sequences **95**

and making it difficult for the attack. A common method to address this issue is to teach players how to fully utilise the basketball court/space. In a 5V5 game, we could use "Head–Hands–Feet" and "Triangle" in a 3V3 situation.

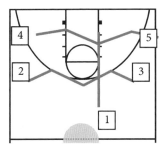 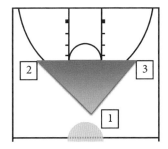

5V5 Head-Hands-Feet   3V3 Triangle

To initiate the attack, player 2 or 3 could do a v-cut draw the opponent into the 3-point line first and sprint out to receive a pass from player 1.

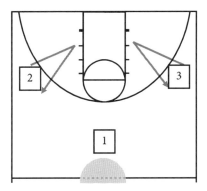

V-cut to receive a pass

Teaching Points:

1. spread around the perimeter,
2. occupy the head, hands, and two feet,
3. cut must go into the "heart" (the key) and run out quickly to occupy one of those unoccupied position.

Suggested Activities:

1. use cones to mark out the areas,
2. have students/players practice different kind of movements (cutting, passing, and receiving) using the actual court,
3. begins with 3s, 4s and 5s progressive,
4. use the space at the half court line for players to practice similar movements while waiting for their turns for maximum participation if the size of the group is too big.

Pass and cut (Give and Go)

Pass and cut is the simplest play in basketball. It involves a player passing the ball to his/her teammate, then cuts to the basketball looking for a return pass from him/her.

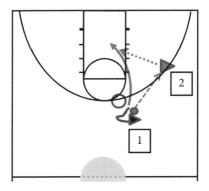

Player 1 passes to player 2, fakes to his right, then follows his pass for a return pass from player 2 for a layup shot.

Suggested Activities:

1. practice 2V0 with both sides before moving to 2V1,
2. students/players who are able to execute the move with a target, e.g. score 5 basketball will move on to play 2V2 game,
3. repeat the activities for 3 players as follows:

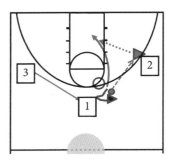
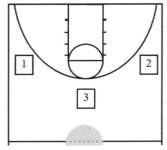

Progress to having 4–5 players eventually. It is important to include the number of defenders progressive to make the task manageable for the attackers.

Screening

The screen is one of the basic methods to free an attacking player from a defensive guard. It is extremely useful in certain types of team offence particularly against a man-to-man defence.

A screen may be described as a legal means of obstructing the path of a defensive player who is attempting to follow his correct defensive path in relation to the offensive player. This is usually done by placing a player in the path which the defensive player requires to follow his opponent to keep in his guarding position; thereby forcing the defensive player to change course, or to go around the screen. This gives the offensive player a distance or position advantage. It must be stressed that a proper screen has to be set in order not to commit a foul.

Teaching Points:

1. screens may be set up at the side of stationary opponents,
2. "blind screens" are set up behind an opponent, i.e. out of the field of vision, and must be set at least

one metre from the opponent. The screener may face in any direction,
3. if a screen is set up on a moving opponent, then the speed of the opponent's movement must be taken into consideration. This means that the screen would have to be set from three to six feet from the moving opponent,
4. once a screen has been set up, the screener may not move except in the same direction and path as his opponent,
5. once a screen has been legally set up, if the screener moves towards the opponent and contact occurs, he has committed a blocking foul,
6. if the screen is legally set, and used, and a defender is "picked-off", the defender has committed a charging foul on the screener.

Common Mistake	Consequence	Remediation
Narrow base Incorrect position.	Unable to block opponent successfully to free up teammate.	Feet shoulder width, crossed arms. Chest to opponent's shoulder formed 90 degree angle (side screen).
Moving screen.	Committed violation on illegal screen.	Once screening position is established, no movement is allowed.

Suggested Activities:

1. in pairs, one player in stationary position, the other player attempt to set a "side" and "back" screen. Change over role,
2. in pairs, one player acts as an attacker in a moving position. The other player anticipates the path of the movement, set up the screen in advance to "block" the path legally,
3. 2 V 1 Game. Practice "Pass and Screen" on the ball side. Attacker read the defence and use skills learned previously e.g. jab step and drive, jab step and shoot for offence,
4. progress to 2 V 2 Game. Screen on ball side,
5. progress to 4 V 2 and 4 V 4 Game with the options of setting screen on or off the ball side.

Pass and screen

Player A passes to player B and sets a screen at the side of player B's defender. Player B uses the correct offensive footwork and dribbles past the screen closely and a quick layup or open shot.

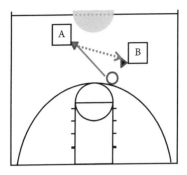

Pick-and-roll

The pick-and-roll is a basic play that involves two offensive players working together, one of them has the ball. It can be used anywhere on the court and is highly effective against defenders playing very close to offensive players. A pick is the act of stopping or blocking the defensive player whereby the defensive player is forced to either run into the teammate or try to move around him. A pick is set for a teammate who dribbles by it for an outside shot, drive, or pass. When the off-the-ball defender switches over to guard the dribblers, the picker spin on the foot farthest from the basket and move toward the basket, looking to receive a return pass from the dribbler for a layup. This is called a roll.

When a pick is set, it is important to use at least two dribbles going by the pick to create space for a pass to the picker who rolls to the basket after the off-the-ball defender switches defence.

102 *Basketball: A Guide for Physical Education Teachers*

Teaching Points:

Preparation Phase:

1. screener sets pick with wide stance (spread legs) and elbows crossed,
2. player with the ball waits for the pick to be set,
3. dribbler observe the defence.

Execution Phase:

1. player with the ball drives off pick hip-to-hip,
2. take at least two dribbles past the pick to create space,
3. dribbler drive for a layout if the "off-the-ball" defender does not switch defence,
4. if the "off-the-ball" defender switches defence, picker rolls (pivot on the outside foot — face the direction in which the dribbler moves) to basket.

Follow-Through Phase:

1. dribbler bounce (or lob) pass to picker rolling to basket.

Common Mistake	Consequence	Remediation
Narrow base Incorrect position.	Unable to block opponent successfully to free up teammate.	Feet shoulder width, crossed arms. Chest to opponent's shoulder formed

(Continued)

Basketball: A Guide for Physical Education Teachers

(Continued)

Common Mistake	Consequence	Remediation
		90 degree angle (side screen). Start dribble only when the screen is properly set.
Dribble off the ball before the screen is set. Dribble too far off the screen.		Dribble close to the screen — hip to hip.
Failed to "roll" after teammate dribbles past the "pick" (screen).	Limit attacking option to only one player to dribble for layup for shoot.	Pivot or roll with the chest facing teammate, break away with a V-shape to create space for passing.
Pivot or "roll" in wrong direction.	Unable to block the opponent before the back.	Roll or pivot with the foot away from the teammate with good eyes contact.

Suggested Activities:

1. ask players to jog and run around the court. Jump stop and land with both feet, pivot using either foot and continue jogging or running,
2. same as above. Cross-arm upon landing. Pivot with one foot, stretch hand to signal for ball (receive a pass),
3. in groups of 3's, two attackers and one defender. Practice 2 V 1 pick and roll,

4. play 4 V 2 and 3 V 3 pick and roll games. Limit dribbling options — e.g. unless for a layup shot, dribble of the screen and shoot or dribble and pass to teammate for shooting/scoring option.

Play 3 V 3 games with the options of using pick and roll or setting screens on or off the ball. Control the dribbling options first to discourage players from dribbling the ball unnecessarily.

Fast break

Fast break is one of the easier ways to score during the transition offence. It is important that the fast break is organized and executed effectively. Good communication, speed and sound fundamentals are essentials.

Teaching Points:

1. fight hard for the ball from rebound, out of bounds, (end line after a basket, and sideline after a violation), jump ball, and interception,
2. counter-offence fast,
3. make accurate passes,
4. spreads the offence by having three lanes (left, centre, and right) covered,
5. reach out for the ball and always pass to the "free" teammate in better position to score.

Common Mistake	Consequence	Remediation
Lack of communication.	Inaccurate passes resulting to slower speed or missed passes.	Signal and ask for the ball.
Did not spread out to cover the three lanes.	Easier for the defenders to intercept the ball or slowed down the offence limit attacking option to only one player to dribble for layup for shoot.	Spread out and cover the three lanes.
Hesitate on attack.	No advantage of having more offenders than defenders.	Head up and eyes open. Read the defence and make quick decision. Player with the ball must be ready to shoot, pass, or dribble.

Suggested Activities:

1. in pairs, practice "outlet" and "fast break". See diagram.

Variation 1: (2V0)

1. player A self-toss and rebounds for the ball. Player 2 shouts for outlet pass, dribbles the ball and takes up the centre lane,

2. player 1 runs behind player 2 and takes up the side lane. Player 2 curves in at the "block" area for a return pass from player B for a layup shot,
3. change role and advance the ball back,

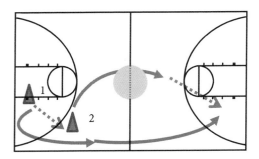

4. in 3's. Same arrangement with the inclusion of player 3. See diagram.

Variation 2: (3V0)

1. same arrangements as the activity mentioned above,
2. player 3 will run straight (taking on the opposite side lane) once the outlet pass has been made,
3. player at the centre lane will have two options to pass the ball,
4. player at the centre picks up the rebound and decides where he wants to start the attack back. Players 2 and 3 cross the baseline and switch position,

108 *Basketball: A Guide for Physical Education Teachers*

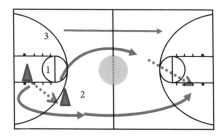

5. practice half court 2 V 1. Player 3 is the defender. Change over after each attack — either scored or defender gets the ball,

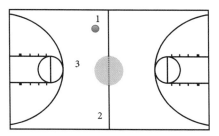

6. practice 3 V 2 drills from the half court. Players 1, 2, and 3 are attackers. Change over when the attackers scored a basketball or defenders get the ball,

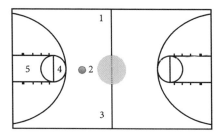

7. extend the games to full court. Form three rows near baseline. Start the ball like the 3V0 drill for the attackers. The two defenders (4 and 5) will station at the front court,
8. next wave of attack will start once the ball is either intercepted by the defenders of a successful basketball made,
9. players 2 and 3 become defenders while players 1, 4, and 5 will job back near the sideline to join the rows,

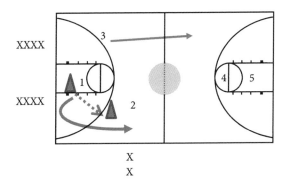

10. combine the drill of 3 V 2 and 2 V 1 (full court),
11. attackers form three rows behind the baseline. Two defenders at the front court in stagger position,
12. player 1 passes ball to 2 or 3, and receives a return pass from them. The three players stay on their lane till front court,

13. apply the half court 3 on 2 offensive strategy,
14. increase the demand (e.g. shorten the given to attackers),

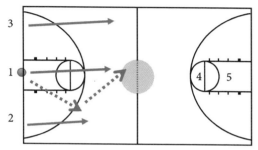

15. once a successful basket is made or players 4 or 5 got the rebound, they will start a 2 on 1 transition offence,
16. player 1 will be the defender and must run back quickly for the defence.

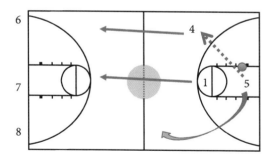

Man-to-man offence

Man-to-man is the original strategy used in Basketball. The principle is very simple, that is, each defensive player on a team is responsible for guarding a specific player of the offensive team. The advantages and disadvantages for man-to-man are:

Advantages:

1. definite responsibility for each player, a definite man to guard throughout the game,
2. possible to match opponents for size, speed, and ability by assigning proper defensive player,
3. it is easy to see who is falling down on, and provide help when necessary,
4. it is the only choice to use when the team is behind the score and game time is running out,
5. it makes a faster and better game pace for spectators.

Disadvantages:

1. the defence is weak against screens,
2. in switching, the player's abilities may not be matched,
3. slow change from to attack (sometimes slow to spot change of possession),
4. requires more actions and skills to play man-to-man properly,
5. it is easy to draw fouls,
6. it is very physically demanding.

There is no doubt that man-to-man requires higher levels of fitness and ability. Some teachers/coaches claim this is an advantage, and others see it as a disadvantage. When a team is behind and it is necessary to speed up the pace of the game, it may be necessary to play man-to-man. In any one-on-one situation, the defensive player is in fact in a man-to-man situation; therefore individually, every player must be able to play with man-to-man principles. These are the general principles governing man-to-man:

1. take responsibility seriously,
2. change of possession at critical time. Get back on quickly,
3. keep between your opponent and the basket,
4. watch the ball as well as opponent (peripheral vision).

Principles by which one plays man-to-man, in addition to the general principles:

1. try to get all players into area of "D" as soon as possible,
2. first two men back may have to prevent or stall the fast break by using horizontal or vertical shuttle,
3. press dribbler to delay fast break,
4. be ready to pick up men as they cross the half-way line.

A team will normally play a sagging man-to-man. This means that they pick up their opponents as they cross the half-way line, guard them loosely until they have the ball or are in the shooting area. The reason for this loose position is that it gives greater protection against screens and the pass-and-cut plays and enables you to see the ball.

The key to break man-to-man is to be able to stay "clam" and handle the pressure well.

Teaching Points:

1. counter-offence by launching fast break and try to score before the defence is set up,
2. use simple 2 V 2 or 3 V 3 options, e.g. Give & Go, Pick & Roll should the fast break fails,
3. use screens, e.g. on the ball or off the ball side may be useful,
4. know your rebounding responsibilities and go for every ball.

Motion Offence

Motion offence uses the concepts of players movements (pass and cut, movements with or without ball), individual skills (dribbling, passing, shooting), and floor spacing for attack. Most commonly set-up for a play is 5-out (5 players stay outside the perimeter and spread-out, 4 out 1 in (4 players stay outside the perimeter and one player stations at the low post). Other formation such as 3 out 2 in is also possible.

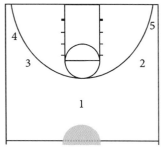

5 Out Formation   4 Out 1 in Formation

Teaching Points:
Movement without Dribble:

1. pass and cut,
2. fill the space.

On Dribbler:

1. go at the defender's hips/shoulders,
2. be a scorer first,
3. get both feet inside the key on penetration,
4. use of shot and foot fakes to create penetration opportunities.

On Receivers:

1. move in and occupy the two (out of the four) keyways,

Suggested Teaching/Coaching Sequences **115**

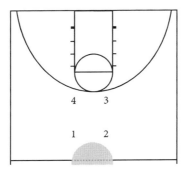

5 out Formation Offence

2. using basis concept of Give and Go,
3. player 1 makes a pass to player 2, cut towards basket for a return pass,
4. the rest of the offensive players rotate and fill the space,
5. player 2 can make a pass to 1 or 3 for a layup or shot from parameter,

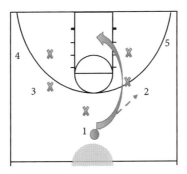

6. using Pick and Roll/Screen,
7. player 1 makes a pass to player 2, and set up a pick,

116 *Basketball: A Guide for Physical Education Teachers*

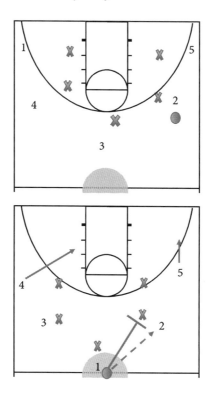

8. player 2 uses the pick and drive towards the basket for a shot or pass to teammates (players 4 or 5) whoever is open,
9. player 1 could roll to fill the space next to player 5 after the pick,
10. the rest of the players fill the open space.

Basic Defensive Team Tactics

Man-to-Man defence

At times when you wish to put pressure on your opponents, you may switch to a "press". This requires you to guard your opponent aggressively and closely at all times. If you pick up the man for close guarding at the half-way line, it is called a half-court press. If you pick up your man as soon as the ball is passed in from under your opponents basket, it is called a full-court press. The objectives of the man-to-man press are:

1. try to gain possession,
2. to create confusion in the opposition,
3. to make a team hurry its passes and make mistakes,
4. to speed up the tempo of the game.

Teaching Points:

1. the defensive concept can be applied for half court or full court,
2. players who are far away from the ball should move to "split line" position whereby they are able to see both the ball and their immediate opponents (triangle defence),
3. defender who is closest to the ball should apply pressure to the immediate opponent,

4. always adjust position according to the ball movement.

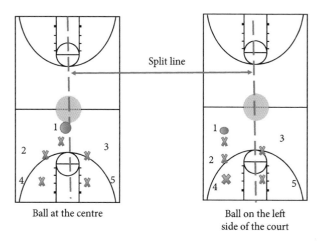

Ball at the centre   Ball on the left side of the court

Defending screens (On-ball)

Defender marking player 3 can opt for 1 going "under" or "over" the screen set by player 3 and stick to the same attacker 1.

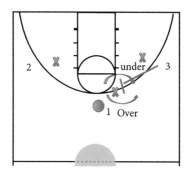

If the option of staying with the same attacker is not possible due to a very screen set by 3, defender guarding player 1 will call for a "switch". He will now be guarding player 3.

Defending screens (Off the ball)

The concept is similar to on ball screen. The only difference is that the screen is now happening away from the ball.

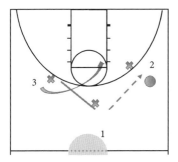

Player 1 makes a pass to 2, and set a screen for 3 to receive a return pass from player 2 for a layup shot.

If the layup option is not available, a shot can be taken immediately after the screen if he is free.

Defending 3 on 2 situation

3 on 2 situation usually happens during quick transition offence. The attackers are able to move the ball from backcourt to frontcourt quickly. To defend the opponents successfully under such unfavourable situation, the defenders should aim to slow down the attackers, with the hope that the rest of the teammates will join them quickly.

Teaching Points:

1. stand in stagger position,
2. first defender force player 1 to make the pass,
3. once the pass has been made, second defender moves and defend the player with ball,
4. the other defender move to the split line and maintain position where man-ball-man can be observed.

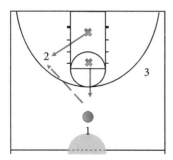 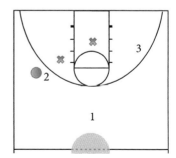

Defending 2 on 1 situation

Activities:
Variation 1:

1. form 3 rows at the half court,
2. ball at the centre line,
3. attackers move and attack the basket,
4. when a pass is made, the attacker with the ball must hold for 3 seconds (timing can be determined by the teacher/coach) to allow the defenders to get use to the alternate defending movement,
5. the attack will be over when (1) successful basket is made or (2) defenders intercepted or rebounded the ball,
6. attackers 2 and 3 (players at the outer lines i.e. left and right sides) will become defenders when there is a changeover of defence and offence,
7. manipulate the time for the ball carrier — the longer the time allowed, the easier for the defenders to adjust their position for defence.

Variation 2:

1. same as above,
2. attackers can make the pass anytime they deem appropriate.

122 *Basketball: A Guide for Physical Education Teachers*

Variation 3:

1. start ball from any place near the half court,
2. attackers do not have to stay in their own lane (left, centre, right),
3. manipulate the time for the attackers to make an attempt (e.g. 8 seconds),
4. shorten the attacking time to increase the difficulty of the task,
5. set a team goal/target or time to common the task.

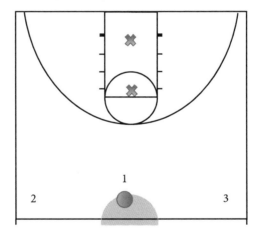

CHAPTER SEVEN
FIBA 3 × 3: Modified Game

FIBA 3 × 3 is a modified game from a standard 5 vs 5 game. It started in the year 2010 as an official game format in the first Youth Olympic Games held in Singapore. It is a 3-on-3 game with the emphasis of individual skills and played at a faster pace. It also incorporated elements of entertainment and excitement by having music and DJ during games at high human traffic areas such as shopping malls.

FIBA 3 × 3: Rules of the Game

Court and Ball: A regular 3 × 3 court playing surface is 15 m (width) × 11 m (length). The official 3 × 3 ball shall be used in all categories.

Team roster: 4 players 3 + 1 substitute.

Referee(s): 1 or 2.

Time/Score keeper(s): Up to 2.

Time-outs: 1 per team, at first dead ball after 6:59 and 3:59 dead ball, 30 seconds.

Initial possession: Coin flip.

Note: The team that wins the coin flip decides whether it takes the ball or leaves it, in order to get it in a potential overtime.

Scoring: 1 point and 2 points, if scored behind the arc.

Game duration and Score limit: 1 × 10 minutes, playing time score limit: 21 points. Applies to regular playing time only.

Note: If a game clock is not available, running time length and sudden death score is at organizer's discretion. FIBA recommends setting score limit in line with the game duration (10 minutes/10 points; 15 minutes/15 points; 21 minutes/21 points).

Overtime: First team to score two (2) points wins the game.

Shot clock: 12 seconds.

Note: If a shot clock device is not available, referee to warn and count down the 5 last seconds.

Free throw(s) following a shooting foul: 1 free throw; 2 free throws, if foul committed behind the arc.

Foul limit per team: 6 team fouls.

Penalty for team fouls 7, 8, and 9: 2 free throws.

Penalty for team fouls 10 and more: 2 free throws + ball possession.

Penalty for technical foul: 1 Free throw, no change of possession.

Penalty for unsportsmanlike foul: 2 Free throws (+ ball possession as of team foul 10 and more). Counted as if 2 fouls for team fouls purposes.

Penalty for disqualifying foul: 2 free throws + ball possession. Counted as if 2 fouls for team fouls purposes.

Possession following a successful goal: Defence possession. Right underneath the hoop. Ball to be dribbled or passed to a player behind the arc. Defensive team not allowed to play for the ball inside the "no-charge semicircle" area underneath the basket.

Following a dead ball: Check ball exchange behind the arc (at the top).

Following a defensive rebound or steal: Ball to be dribbled/passed behind the arc.

Following a jump ball situation: Defence possession.

Substitutions: In dead ball situations, prior to the check ball. The substitute can enter the game after his teammate steps off the court and establishes a physical contact with him behind the end line opposite the basket. Substitutions require no action from the referees or table officials.

Notes: *A player is considered to be "behind the arc" if neither of his feet are inside nor step the arc **Official FIBA Basketball Rules apply for all game situations not specifically mentioned above ***Refer to 3 × 3 Rules of the Game text version for standings, default, forfeits, protests, and disqualification.

Information Taken from ©FIBA, January 2019.

What are the key differences between FIBA 3 × 3 & FIBA 5-on-5 game?
The key differences include: Speed-in execution (long vs short playing sequences), pace of the game, emphasis on "one-on-one" game, emphasis on instinctive (3 × 3) vs team strategy (5-on-5) and increased spacing for 3-on-3.

What are the advantages of FIBA 3 × 3?
The advantages include: It is a simplified version of the normal game, it needs less infrastructure and less players, it is attractive for kids and younger players, it is a tool for players' development and tool for teams' set plays development.

CHAPTER EIGHT
Samples of Basketball Skills Rubric

There are many different ways to assess the skill levels of the players. Teachers can use rubrics for qualitative analysis of the skill levels (beginners, intermediate, proficient, and expert) or objective scores such as number of repetitions or basket scored. We provide three examples here.

Fundamental Basketball Skills

Rating of 1–6 can represent Lowest to Highest skill level or it can be changed to 4 levels (Basic, Adequate, Proficient, Advanced).

128 Basketball: A Guide for Physical Education Teachers

						A. Ball Handling: Dribbling
1	2	3	4	5	6	1. Head up
1	2	3	4	5	6	2. Dribble waist high or lower
1	2	3	4	5	6	3. Protection on ball
1	2	3	4	5	6	4. Firm pump-handle dribble
1	2	3	4	5	6	5. Finger-tip control
1	2	3	4	5	6	6. All above with non-dominant hand
						B. Ball Handling: Passing
1	2	3	4	5	6	1. See floor-not tunnel vision
1	2	3	4	5	6	2. Quick firm passes
1	2	3	4	5	6	3. Hits open man immediately
						C. Ball Handling: Receiving Pass
1	2	3	4	5	6	1. Works to get open for pass
1	2	3	4	5	6	2. Step and reach to meet the pass
1	2	3	4	5	6	3. Triple threat position
1	2	3	4	5	6	4. Protects the ball
						D. Rebounding (Offensive)
1	2	3	4	5	6	1. Getting inside position
1	2	3	4	5	6	2. Body position (legs bent, hands up, elbows out)
1	2	3	4	5	6	3. Second and third effort
1	2	3	4	5	6	4. Timing
						E. Rebounding (Defensive)
1	2	3	4	5	6	1. Blocking out
1	2	3	4	5	6	2. Going to boards
1	2	3	4	5	6	3. Wide base when landing and protection of ball
1	2	3	4	5	6	4. Outlet pass

(*Continued*)

	F. Defence
1 2 3 4 5 6	1. Keep feet spread
1 2 3 4 5 6	2. Helps on defence
1 2 3 4 5 6	3. Play an aggressive defence
1 2 3 4 5 6	4. Hands up
	G. Body Balance
1 2 3 4 5 6	1. Move under control
1 2 3 4 5 6	2. Feet shoulder width
1 2 3 4 5 6	3. Hands waist high
1 2 3 4 5 6	4. Head on a mid-point between both feet

Technique Assessment Use Rubrics

You can assess individual skills based on players'/students' demonstrations of the one-handed set shot, a layup, and rebounding. Illustration and descriptors for the one-handed set shot, a layup, and rebounding (adapted from Wissel, 2011).

Rebounding (Without Opponent)

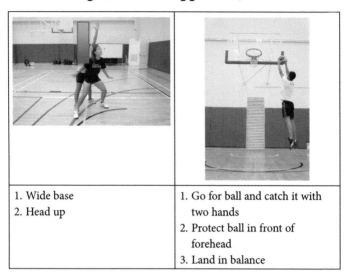

1. Wide base 2. Head up	1. Go for ball and catch it with two hands 2. Protect ball in front of forehead 3. Land in balance

Scoring for Rebounding

Student will perform the technique three times and each performance will be scored using the rubric below. A maximum of 3 points can be scored for each performance, and a maximum of 9 points can be scored for this section of the technique assessment.

Points	0	1	2	3
Description	Student performs none of the descriptors.	Student performs 1–2 descriptors.	Student performs 3–4 descriptors.	Student performs all 5 descriptors.

One-Handed Set Shot

1. Feet shoulder-width apart 2. Knees slightly bent 3. Shoulders relaxed 4. Elbow in 5. Shooting hand faces basket; non-shooting hand supports ball 6. Ball high between ear and shoulder 7. Eyes on basket	1. Lower knees before shot 2. Eyes on target	1. Extend legs, back, shoulders and elbow together 2. Keep non-shooting hand on ball until release 3. Flex shooting hand's wrist and fingers forward 4. Release ball off finger pads 5. Follow through with arm extended 6. Ball enters basket

Scoring for One-Handed Set Shot

Student will perform the technique three times and each performance will be scored using the rubric below. A maximum of 5 points can be scored for each performance, and a maximum of 15 points can be scored for this section of the technique assessment.

Points	0	1	2	3	2
Description	Student performs none of the descriptors.	Student performs 1–7 descriptors.	Student performs 8–13 descriptors.	Student performs all 14 descriptors.	Ball enters basket.

Samples of Basketball Skills Rubric 133

Layup

1. Pick up ball at knee of shooting side foot; shooting hand on top, non-shooting hand supports ball 2. Take short step with take-off foot 3. Dip knee of take-off foot 4. Eyes on basket	1. Raise ball straight up to shoot with shooting hand facing basket 2. Jump straight up, pushing off with take-off foot 3. Protect ball with non-shooting hand until release 4. Land in balance at spot of take-off, ready to rebound 5. Ball enters basket

Scoring for Layup

Student will perform the technique three times and each performance will be scored using the rubric below. A maximum of 5 points can be scored for each performance, and a maximum of 15 points can be scored for this section of the technique assessment.

Points	0	1	2	3	2
Description	Student performs none of the descriptors.	Student performs 1–4 descriptors.	Student performs 5–7 descriptors.	Student performs all 8 descriptors.	Ball enters basket.

Gameplay Assessment Use Rubrics

You can assess the gameplay performance of players/students using rubrics. The concepts and its related behaviours are detailed in the table below, and the performance is rated on a 5-point scale ranging from "very effective (always)" to "very ineffective (never)".

Concepts	Behaviours (adapted from Basketball learning outcomes; SDCD, 2016)	Very effective (always)	Effective (usually)	Moderately effective (sometimes)	Ineffective (rarely)	Very ineffective (never)
Keeping possession of the ball	• Pass the ball when guarded to a teammate who is free, dodge the defender and move into open space to receive the ball. • Dodge the defender and move into open space, receive the ball with a jump/stride stop and pivot to a ready position to shoot, pass or dribble.					

(*Continued*)

Concepts	Behaviours (adapted from Basketball learning outcomes; SDCD, 2016)	Very effective (always)	Effective (usually)	Moderately effective (sometimes)	Ineffective (rarely)	Very ineffective (never)
Using space to invade	• Receive the ball in a ready position to shoot, pass or dribble, and dribble when there is an open lane towards the basket.					
Creating space to invade	• Dodge the defender and move into open space to create options for teammate to shoot, pass or dribble.					
Attacking the goal	• Receive the ball in a ready position to shoot, dribble or shoot, shoot when there is space and within range and ability, and follow through to rebound the ball. • Dribble when there is an open lane towards the basket, shoot in a continuous action when within range and ability, and follow through to rebound the ball.					

(*Continued*)

(*Continued*)

Concepts	Behaviours (adapted from Basketball learning outcomes; SDCD, 2016)	Very effective (always)	Effective (usually)	Moderately effective (sometimes)	Ineffective (rarely)	Very ineffective (never)
Regaining possession of the ball	• Intercept the pass when it is within the defender's reach. • Rebound the ball after a shot.					
Delaying the invasion	• Guard the attacker to prevent the attacker from dribbling towards the basket.					
Denying space to invade	• Guard the attacker to prevent the attacker from receiving the ball.					
Denying scoring opportunities	• Guard the attacker to prevent the attacker from shooting.					

CHAPTER NINE
Sample Lesson Plans

Sample Lesson Plan 1

Duration: 1 h 30 min
Total no. of pupils: 40
Equipment: 20 basketballs, 20 cones, bids

Lesson Focus:
1. Ball handling
2. Passing

Lesson Objectives:
1. Able to be comfortable handling a basketball.
2. Able to execute 10 successful chest passes to a stationary partner over a distance of 5 metres.
3. Able to execute 10 successful bounce passes to a stationary partner over a distance of 5 metres.

140 *Basketball: A Guide for Physical Education Teachers*

4. Able to execute 10 successful overhead passes to a stationary partner over a distance of 5 metres.
5. Able to apply skills learnt in a modified basketball game.

Time	Activity	Organisation/ Space	Teaching Points	Remarks
5 minutes	*Activity 1: Ball Handling (warm-up)*			
	1. Students will get in pairs, each pair with one basketball.			
	2. One student picks up the basketball and performs a ball handing move. The partner will observe carefully and will try to repeat the same move.			
	3. If he/she is able to follow exactly, she will be rewarded a point.			
	4. Switch roles after each turn.			

Note: If the duration for a lesson is shorter, teacher/coach can reduce the skill/concept taught and yet is able to follow the flow of the lesson plan.

Sample Lesson Plans 141

Time	Activity	Organisation/Space	Teaching Points	Remarks
10 minutes	(1) *Figure of Eight Leg Wrap* 1. Feet wide apart 2. Ball is moved in a "figure of eight" action around the legs 3. Change direction of the ball's movement 4. Count the number of successful catch within a time limit	1. Students get in pairs 2. Each pair shares a basketball	1. Use finger pads only 2. Keep heads and eyes up, look front 3. Maintain a balanced stance, feet shoulder width apart. Wider stance if necessary	Instructor will monitor the students and based on his/her discretion to conduct variation activities

(*Continued*)

(Continued)

Time	Activity	Organisation/Space	Teaching Points	Remarks
	Variation 1: 1. Dribble the ball in a "figure of eight" action around the legs 2. Change direction 3. Count the number of successful dribbles complete within a time limit *Variation 2:* 1. Keep knees straightened 2. Bounce the ball in a "figure of eight" action around the legs			If students are not able to cope with the main activity it is alright to leave out the variation activities

(2) *Straddle Flip*
   1. Feet wide apart
   2. Hold the ball with both hands in front between the legs
   3. Flip the ball into the air and catch the ball again with two hands behind the legs before it hits the ground
   4. Count the number of successful catch within a time limit

Variation 1:
   1. Start with holding the ball between the legs

1. Students will get in pairs
2. Each pair shares a basketball

1. Use finger pads only
2. Keep heads and eyes up, look front
3. Maintain a balanced stance, feet shoulder width apart. Wider stance if necessary

(*Continued*)

(Continued)

Time	Activity	Organisation/Space	Teaching Points	Remarks
	2. Flip the ball into the air and catch the ball again by alternating the hands before the ball hits the ground again			
10 minutes	*Activity 2: (3 V 1 Monkey) Modified Game:* 1. Objective of the game is to make at least 10 passes without losing the ball. It includes interception by the "monkey" or losing the ball due to error in passing	1. Four in a playing area 2. Students will be assigned to their respective squares 3. Cones will be place at cross-sectional points to mark out the area 4. Tossers stay stationary, only the "monkey" can move around		

2. Balls that are in flight should not be above the head level and should not touch the ground
3. Once the ball is intercepted, the "monkey" will change roles with the tosser
4. Passers are not allowed to move. Only the "monkey" will be allowed to move

5 minutes Questioning:
1. How did you make a pass? (push the ball straight)

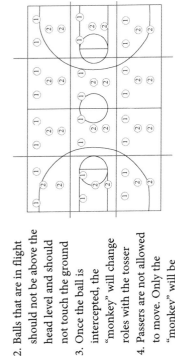

(*Continued*)

146 *Basketball: A Guide for Physical Education Teachers*

(Continued)

Time	Activity	Organisation/Space	Teaching Points	Remarks
	2. How do you make a pass that is easy for your friend to catch, yet it is fast and accurate? (a ball that does not roll during flight, fast and lands near your friend's chest.)			
10 minutes	*Activity 3: Practise task (chest pass)* 1. Students will learn the proper technique to execute a chest pass 2. Students will complete 20 chest passes	1. Students work in pairs	1. Fingers relaxed and spread over the ball (Diamond)	

Sample Lesson Plans **147**

3. Next increase the distance between pairs by asking students to take three steps back
4. Students will have a mini competition to see which pair could finish it in the fastest time

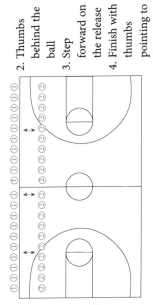

2. Thumbs behind the ball
3. Step forward on the release
4. Finish with thumbs pointing to the ground and fingers pointing towards target
5. Receiver should catch the ball at his/her chest level

(*Continued*)

(Continued)

Time	Activity	Organisation/Space	Teaching Points	Remarks
5 minutes	*Activity 4: (3 V 1 Monkey) Modified Game* 1. Students will get back to the same game 2. Students must try to make at least 10 passes without being intercepted with better chest pass technique	1. Four in a playing area		

| 5 minutes | Activity 5: (3 V 1 Monkey) Modified Game | 1. Four in a group
1. Students will try to make as many passes as possible without losing possession
2. Balls that are in flight should not be above the head level and should touch the ground once
3. Once the ball is intercepted, the interceptor will change roles with the tosser
4. Additional rule. Students now can move about in the squares but only if they do not have the ball |

(Continued)

(Continued)

Time	Activity	Organisation/Space	Teaching Points	Remarks
5 minutes	*Questioning:* 1. How did you make a pass? (called a bounce pass) 2. How do you make a pass that is easy for your friend to catch, yet it is fast and accurate? Where should you bounce the ball? (Bounce a ball that is able to reach your friend's waist level.)			

10 minutes Activity 6: Practice task *(Bounce pass)*
1. Students will learn the proper technique to execute a bounce pass
2. Students will complete 20 times of bounce pass
3. Next increase the distance between pairs
4. Those who are able to do it can precede to single hand bounce passes
5. Students will have a mini competition to see which pair could finish it in the fastest time

1. Students work in pairs

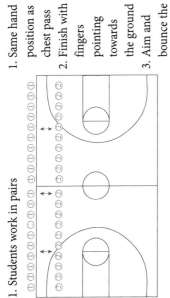

1. Same hand position as chest pass
2. Finish with fingers pointing towards the ground
3. Aim and bounce the ball at two-thirds the distance to receiver

(Continued)

Sample Lesson Plans **151**

(Continued)

Time	Activity	Organisation/Space	Teaching Points	Remarks
			4. The receiver should catch the ball at his/her waist level	
5 *minutes*	*Activity 7: (3 V 1 Monkey) Modified Game* 1. Students will get back to play the game 2. Students must try to make five passes without being intercepted. Only using bounce passes	1. Four in a playing area		

3. After which students are allowed to use either chest or bounce pass
4. Additional rule.
   Students now can move about in the squares but only if they do not have the ball

5 minutes | *Activity 8: Practice task (overhead pass)*
1. Students will learn the proper technique to execute an overhead pass
2. Students will complete 20 times of overhead pass
3. Next increase the distance between pairs

1. Students will work in pairs

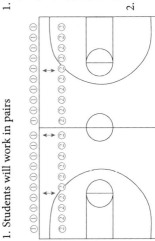

1. Ball held with pads of fingers and upper portion of palm above the forehead
2. Step towards receiver

(Continued)

154 Basketball: A Guide for Physical Education Teachers

(Continued)

Time	Activity	Organisation/Space	Teaching Points	Remarks
	4. Students will have a mini competition to see which pair could finish it in the fastest time		3. Snap wrist to follow through 4. Receiver should still receive the ball at chest height	
10 minutes	Activity 9: *(variation) passing on the move* 1. 2 rows at each lane 2. In pairs they will pass in the move to the half court line 3. The pairs will join their own group from the perimeter	1. 2 groups of 8 players 2. 4 groups of 6 players	1. With ball, maximum two steps 2. Toss ball slightly in front of your friend 3. Receiver can clap	

4. Drills to perform
   a. 2 × chest bounce
   b. 2 × bounce pass
   c. 2 × alternate between chest and bounce pass

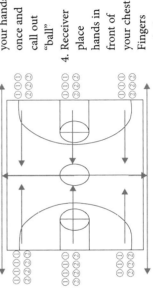

your hands once and call out "ball"

4. Receiver place hands in front of your chest Fingers pointing slightly towards the sky

156 *Basketball: A Guide for Physical Education Teachers*

(Continued)

Time	Activity	Organisation/Space	Teaching Points	Remarks
5 minutes	*Activity 10: Game 5 V 3* 1. Students will play a 5 V 3 2. Attackers will start from the centre line 3. Defenders start from goal line 4. Attackers are to get into the goal line zone with the ball to score a point 5. Score as many points as possible without interception 6. If ball is intercepted, players go back to original starting position. Points go back to zero	1. 8 in a playing area (5 attackers and 3 defenders) 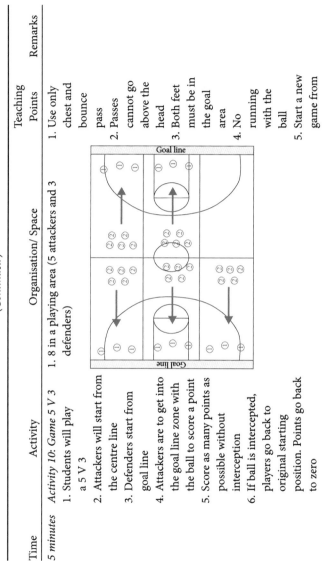	1. Use only chest and bounce pass 2. Passes cannot go above the head 3. Both feet must be in the goal area 4. No running with the ball 5. Start a new game from	

	7. Defender who intercepted the ball will change roles who the person who make the pass 8. After 2 mins all defenders must change roles with attackers	the centre line
5 minutes	*Conclusion* Instructor to recap what was taught in the lesson and the teaching points for the various passes 1. What are the key points of chest pass/bounce pass and overhead?	Refer to all of the above teaching points

Sample Lesson Plans **157**

Sample Lesson Plan 2

Duration: 1 h 30 min
Number of Pupils: 40
Equipment: 20 basketballs, 40 cones, bids

Lesson Focus:
1. Offence: fake, setting screen, and roll.
2. Defence: on the ball, off the ball.

Lesson Objectives:
At the end of the lesson, students should be able to:

1. Use the offensive techniques: fake, screen and roll, as well as the defensive techniques: on the ball and off the ball in the modified game (2 V 2, 4 V 2, or 3 V 3) situations.
2. Articulate when and how to apply the offensive and defensive techniques learned in the modified game situations.
3. Able to work together with classmates in all planned activities during lesson.

Sample Lesson Plans 159

Time	Activity	Organisation/Space	Teaching Points	Remarks
5 minutes	*Warm-up: Foot work* Zig Zag movement: 1. Space out (1 arm length) 2. Zig-zag movement from one end to the end of the court Jump stop, pivot, roll, and move: 1. Same arrangement as above. Students will do a jump stop, pivot to left, and move forward 2. Same arrangement but pivot to the right. Focus on showing palm (to receive ball)	1. 2 rows behind the sideline	1. Bend knees 2. Weight on the foot of opposite direction of move 3. Show palm to receive ball 1. Land with legs shoulder width apart 2. Bend knees (90–100 degree) 3. Cross arms 4. Weight on the ball of the pivot foot	

(*Continued*)

160 *Basketball: A Guide for Physical Education Teachers*

(Continued)

Time	Activity	Organisation/Space	Teaching Points	Remarks
10 minutes	2 V 2 Maintain Possession Game: 1. Students will play 2 V 2 game in a square 2. Change over attack/defence role whenever interception made 3. Man-to-man defence 4. Keep score (1 point = 1 successful pass)	(diagram of squares with 2 V 2 arrangement) 1. In pair 2. 4 player/square	5. Show palm to receive ball 1. No illegal using of hands 2. Play in the playing area	Refer to the pre-lesson videos and materials in the blackboard Watch video on how the game is played
3 minutes	Q & A: Q: Was it easy for the attackers to score points? A: No A: No	1. Sit, listen and response		

Q: Why was it so?
A: Tight/good defence
Q: How to overcome this problem?
A: Find ways to shake off the defender – e.g., fake the defender – e.g., fake
Good, let's practice the skill

4 minutes *Demonstration:*
Fake and move

1. Passer stations at one cone
2. Receiver fakes and moves from one cone to the other
3. Knees bent (90–100 degree)
4. Place body weight on the foot opposite

Refer to the video 2 V 1 fake and creating space

Sample Lesson Plans **161**

(*Continued*)

162 Basketball: A Guide for Physical Education Teachers

(Continued)

Time	Activity	Organisation/Space	Teaching Points	Remarks
			the direction of move	
			5. Push using the ball of the foot and show palm towards direction of move	
			6. Passer sends ball 1 arm ahead of the receiver	
			7. Change over after 20 passes	
10 minutes	*Practice:* Fake and move	1. In paris 2. Stay inside activity 2 playing area	1. Same as above	

Sample Lesson Plans **163**

10 minutes | *Variation 1: 3 V 1 (10 mins)* | 1. In 4s: 3 V 1 | 1. As above | Refer to the video – 2 V 1 fake to create space
| 1. Practice with 1 defender, 1 receiver and 2 passers rotating | | | Proceed to the next activity only when students are able to meet the target set
| 2. Change over the role (made 5 successful passes) in "downward" rotation, i.e. defender becomes the receiver; the receiver moves to the passer's row | Receiver ★ Passer | |

Variation 2: 2v2 line game (10 mins)
1. 2 defenders and 2 attackers

(Continued)

164 *Basketball: A Guide for Physical Education Teachers*

(Continued)

Time	Activity	Organisation/Space	Teaching Points	Remarks
	2. 1 point for each successful attempt 3. 6 points/game 4. Change opponent with next court (winner vs winner)			
3 minutes	Q & A: Q: How to prevent the attackers from making more attempts/goals? A: Apply pressure on and off the ball Q: How? A: Stay close to the attackers Great! There are some rules to follow Let's practice.	1. Sit, listen, and response		

| 4 minutes | *Demonstration:* Defence the fake move | 1. Sit, listen, and response | *On the ball:*
 1. Live: 1.5 arm length
 2. Dribble: 1 arm length, stay close to the attacker
 3. Knees bent (90–100 degree)
 4. Big step for leading foot: pointing to the direction of move
 5. Eyes on the attacker
 Off the ball:
 1. Maintain triangle formation: man-you-ball | Refer to the pre-lesson materials on the blackboard |

(Continued)

(Continued)

Time	Activity	Organisation/Space	Teaching Points	Remarks
			2. Hand-up to stop the pass 3. Knees bent (90–100 degree) and get ready to move	
14 minutes	*Practice:* Defending the fake move (2 V 2) 1. Attacker holds ball for 5 seconds before making the next pass to allow defenders to adjust their position *Progression:* 1. Reduce the holding time to 3 seconds 2. No timing restriction	1. In 4s (2 V 2) 2. Same organisation as 2 V 2 possession game	1. As above	

Sample Lesson Plans **167**

	3. 6 points/game	
	4. Exchange opponents (winner vs winner) with the next court	
3 minutes	Q & A:	1. Sit, listen, and response
	Q: Now that the defenders are more efficient, how to break down the tight defence to score more points?	
	A: Use quick passes or lob pass	
	Q: Are these good solutions?	
	A: May be intercepted by the defenders due to tight defence.	

(Continued)

(Continued)

Time	Activity	Organisation/Space	Teaching Points	Remarks
	We could create some moves to free up our teammate, and save energy for better attack options. Let's try!			
4 minutes	*Demonstration:* Setting screen & roll	1. Sit, listen, and response	1. Set up screen at the side of a stationary opponent (perpendicular-90 degree) 2. Feet shoulder width apart, cross arms 3. Knees bent (90–100 degrees)	Refer to the pre-lesson materials in the blackboard

4. Attacker with ball adopts triple threads position
5. Once a screen has been set up, attacker dribbles pass the screen (hip-to-hip), and go for the basket
6. Screener faces the teammate/ball and rolls/moves (pivot) toward the basket to support

(Continued)

170 *Basketball: A Guide for Physical Education Teachers*

(Continued)

Time	Activity	Organisation/Space	Teaching Points	Remarks
15 minutes	*Practice:* Setting screen & roll:	1. In 2s, practice screen and roll inside the grid area (side line to side line) 2. Practice screening on both sides of the defender	1. As above: without ball	
	Progression: 2 V 2	1. In 4s, practice 2 V 2 screen and roll. Defender near the ball adopts passive defence 2. Change over when attacking team reaches the other end of the line. 6 points/game	1. As above: with ball	
	6 V 2	1. 6 V 2 line game: Extend the playing area. 6 points/game using screen and role only. Rotate roles thereafter		
	5 V 3	2. 5 V 3 line game: 8 points/game. Change opponents with the next court		

| 5 minutes | Closure | Q: What have we learned today?
A: Fake to create space for better support and attack.
Q: How to do that?
A: Refer to the teaching points

Q: What else can we do?
A: Setting good screen: refer to the teaching points | 1. Bend knees
2. Weight on opposite direction of move
3. Show palm to receive ball

1. Set up screen at the side of a stationary opponent (perpendicular-90 degree)
2. Feet shoulder width apart, cross arms
3. Knees bent (90–100 degrees) |

(Continued)

(Continued)

Time	Activity	Organisation/Space	Teaching Points	Remarks
			4. Once a screen has been set up, attacker dribbles pass the screen (hip-to-hip), and go for the basket	
			5. Screener faces the teammate/ball and rolls/moves (pivot) toward the basket to support	

Q: What about the one with the ball?
A: Refer to the teaching points

1. In triple threads position
2. Wait for the screen to be set Once a screen has been set up, attacker dribbles pass the screen (hip-to-hip), and go for the basket

Q: Great! How to stop the fake move employs by the attackers?
A: Refer to the teaching points

On the ball:
1. Live: 1.5 arm distance
2. Dribble: 1 arm distance, stay close
3. Knees bent (90–100 degrees)

(Continued)

(Continued)

Time	Activity	Organisation/Space	Teaching Points	Remarks
			4. Big step for leading foot: pointing to the direction of move 5. Eyes on the attacker *Off the ball*: 1. Maintain triangle: man-you-ball 2. Hand-up to stop the pass 3. Knees bent (90–100 degrees) and get ready to move	

References

American Sport Education Program (2007). *Coaching Youth Basketball* (4th Ed.). United States: Human Kinetics.

Griffin, L. L., Mitchell, S. A. and Oslin, J. L. (1997). *Teaching Sport Concepts and Skills: A Tactical Games Approach.* Champaign, IL: Human Kinetics.

Koh, K. T. and Teo, H. H. (2003). *National Coaching Accreditation Programme — Level 1 Coaching Manual (Technical).* Basketball Association of Singapore.

Koh, K. T., Lee, K. S., Tan, M. T. and Teo, H. H. (2006). *Basketball Skills Test Manual.* Ministry of Education, Singapore.

Koh, K. T., Teo, H. H., Wang, C. K. J. and Mah, S. S. (2007). *Integrated Level 1 Basketball Coaching Course.* Basketball Association of Singapore.

Launder, A. G. (2001). *Play Practice*, Champaign, IL: Human Kinetics.

SDCD. (2016). Physical Education Teaching and Learning Syllabus: Primary, Secondary and Pre-University. Retrieved from https://www.moe.gov.sg/docs/default-source/document/

education/syllabuses/physical-sports-education/files/physical_education_syllabus_2014.pdf.

WABC. (2018). Level 1 Coaching Manual. Retrieved from https://wabc.fiba.com/manual/level-1/l1-coach/l1-1-roles-and-values/l1-1-1-leadership/.

Wissel, H. (2011). *Basketball: Steps to Success* (3rd Ed.). Champaign, IL: Human Kinetics.

Wright, S., McNeill, M., Fry, J. and Wang, J. (2005). Teaching teachers to play and teach games. *Physical Education and Sport Pedagogy,* **10**: 61–82.

Congratulatory Notes

It all begins from the love of basketball. Having known Dr. Koh through basketball for many years, I can testify to his tremendous passion and commitment for basketball. Many of us in the basketball circle would concur with me that Dr. Koh has made tremendous contribution to the development of basketball in Singapore. He is truly one of the many basketball advocates in Singapore that I deeply admire.

We can be assured that this publication will be an excellent training resource for physical education teachers and basketball coaches. Many students and athletes will greatly benefit from it.

Wishing him every success as we look forward to Dr. Koh's unceasing contribution towards the growth and developmental of basketball in Singapore.

Hoo Boon Hock,
President, Basketball Association of Singapore (BAS),
Vice President, Southeast Asia Basketball Association
(SEABA)

The game of Basketball is a wonderful vehicle for developing the general physical education skills of body movement fundamentals, passing, catching, understanding principles of creating space, moving into space, timing of movement and team values and principles of play. Of course, for participants to enjoy playing the game over a long period of time, developing the fundamental skills for Basketball is essential. This book will be an essential and valuable resource providing a sound base of information for physical education teachers and beginning coaches to not only teach participants the fundamentals, values, and team principles of play but to also enjoy sustained participation in the wonderful game of Basketball. I commend this book to all physical education teachers and beginner coaches.

Zoran Radović
FIBA National Federations and Sport Director

Pedagogy and basketball are joined at the hip from birth!

In fact, it was a Physical Education teacher's "academic" idea in creating an indoor wintertime recreational exercise for his wards that led to the very invention of basketball.

Many winters, and summers, have passed since Dr. James Naismith "tipped off" for the first time at the YMCA in Springfield — way back in 1891. Basketball itself has transcended many a dimension from that nascent idea of a physical indoor exercise to a supremely popular professional sport in the world.

Coaching manuals in basketball too have kept themselves abreast of the developments in the sport, but roots of the very basic principles and values of basketball continue to be guided by the very simple and basic concepts of getting youngsters inducted, and induced, into an activity of enormous, but attractive, physical exertion.

It is very heartening to note that Dr. Koh Koon Teck, Head of Physical Education and Sport Sciences at National Institute of Education-Singapore and a very resourceful coaching instructor in the FIBA family, has set about in an attempt in bringing about this basketball teaching resource book which I am sure will be of great use for basic physical education teachers as well as elite coaches.

I am sure the developmental activities, guided by pedagogical principles, will be a very useful addition to the ever-growing literary resources in the sport of basketball.

I wish him very well in his endeavour. More importantly, I wish this effort is put to good and effective use by its readers in taking the sport basketball wider in reach and deeper in understanding.

Best Wishes to the millions of basketball lovers all over the world.

Hagop Khajirian
FIBA Executive Director, Asia

Dr. Koh Koon Teck and Dr. John Wang are to be congratulated for writing this guide to teaching and coaching the rather complex but wonderful game of basketball. This guide will be particularly helpful to instructors that are not so familiar with the game. This book is well written, and the photographs and diagrams will help those who are visual learners. The guide covers both traditional and game-based approaches, which will be useful to teachers and coaches. The authors' use of hyperlinked sources will also be very helpful to practitioners. Let the games begin!

Steven Wright
Professor, Coordinator of Health and Physical Education, University of New Hampshire, U.S.A.,
Played basketball at the NCAA (U.S.A.) level and coached in the U.S., Europe, and Asia
Secretary General of the International Alliance of Health, Physical Education, Dance, and Sport

Index

A
advantages for man-to-man, 111
advantages of FIBA 3 × 3, 126
athletes' interest, 25

B
back court, 18
backdoor cut, 76
ball handling, 36, 139
basic arm action, 90
basic defensive team tactics, 117
basic floor spacing, 94
basic individual defensive skills, 86
basic individual offensive skills, 42
basic offensive team tactics, 94
basic stance and footwork, 86
behind the back dribble, 64
between the legs, 65
blocking out, 93
bounce pass, 47

C
centre, 8
chest pass, 46
comparison, 30
control dribble, 61

court, 6
crossover dribble, 62

D
defence: on the ball, off the ball, 158
defending 2 on 1 situation, 121
defending 3 on 2 situation, 120
defending screens (off the ball), 119
defending screens (on-ball), 118
disadvantages for man-to-man, 111
double dribble, 18
dribbling, 61
drill-driven, 29
drop step, 90

F
fast break, 105
FIBA 3 × 3, 123
field goal, 14
figure of 8, 37
footwork, 42
free throw (or foul shots), 14–15
fundamental basketball skills, 127

G
game, 26
game concept approach, 23
game length, 11
gameplay assessment use rubrics, 136

H
history, 1

I
inquiry-based teaching approach, 25
interesting facts, 2

J
jab step and drive, 78
jab step and shoot, 80
jump ball, 12–13

K
key differences, 126

L
layup, 70, 134
lesson plan, 139

M
man-to-man defence, 117
man-to-man offence, 110
modified game, 31, 123

motion offence, 113
movements with ball, 78
movements without ball, 74

O
offence: fake, setting screen, and roll, 158
officiating, 19
one-handed set shot, 132
out of court, 13
overhead pass, 48

P
pass and cut, 96
pass and screen, 100
passing, 139
passing and receiving, 46
personal foul, 15
pick-and-roll, 101
pivoting, 44
playing positions, 7
point guard, 7
possession, 13
power forward, 8
protection dribble, 62

Q
question-and-answer session, 27
quick decision-making, 29

R
rebounding, 85, 130
rules, 11, 123

S
screening, 98
set shot, 54
shooting, 53
shooting guard, 7
shot fake and drive, 82
shot fake and shoot, 84
skills rubric, 127
small forward, 8
speed dribble, 64
starting the game, 12
straddle flip, 38
straight cut, 74
substitution, 16

T
tactical awareness, 29
tactical awareness and decision-making skills, 26
teaching/coaching basic, 35
technique assessment use rubrics, 129
time-out, 16
traditional approach, 23

transfer of skill and concept, 28
travelling, 17

W
waist wrap, 40